MW00616383

Ancient Secrets Cookbook

RECIPES
for VIBRANT HEALTH,
UNLIMITED ENERGY &
PEACE of MIND

Carol K. Ray

Wisdom of the World Press

ANCIENT SECRETS COOKBOOK
RECIPES for VIBRANT HEALTH, UNLIMITED ENERGY &
PEACE of MIND
by Carol K. Ray with foreword by Dr. Clint G. Rogers
and Dr. Smita Naram

Published by Wisdom of the World Press
www.MyAncientSecrets.com

ISBN: 978-1-952353-98-7
Book Cover Courtesy of Heidi Aden, Lions Pen:
LionsPenGraphics.com

Printed in the United States

Medical Disclaimer

All content found in this document, printed or electronic, including text, images, audio, or other formats were created for informational purposes only. The Content is not intended to be a substitute for professional medical advice, diagnosis, or treatment. Always seek the advice of your physician or other qualified health provider with any questions you may have regarding a medical condition. Never disregard professional medical advice or delay in seeking it because of something you have read in this document.

If you think you may have a medical emergency, call your doctor, go to the emergency department, or call 911 (or the equivalent in your area) immediately. The Ancient Secrets Foundation does not recommend or endorse any specific tests, physicians, products, procedures, opinions, or other information that may be mentioned in this document. Reliance on any information provided by Ancient Secrets Foundation employees, volunteers, contracted writers, or medical professionals presenting content for publication is solely at your own risk.

"I DID NOT COME TO TEACH YOU, I CAME
TO LOVE YOU, LOVE WILL TEACH YOU."
SIDDHA VEDA MASTER HEALERS

*If you change your food, you
can change your future." -Dr.
Naram (Ancient Secrets of a
Master Healer, p. 172)*

Preface

Dear One

What if there were Ancient Secrets regarding food
choices that could lead you to Vibrant Health,
Unlimited Energy, and Peace of Mind?

What if love guided every choice you
made,ncluding learning how to improve the food
you serve yourself and others?

The book you are holding in your hands right now came from a calling of the heart, inspired by the opening quote of the book, Ancient Secrets of a Master Healer:

"I didn't come to teach you.
I came to love you.
Love will teach you."

Ancient Secrets of a Master Healer – Opening Statement

This cookbook is a manifestation of those in the Ancient Secrets Community who are living that quote. Love is teaching them; love is guiding them. And I believe it was love that guided you here, too.

Take, for example, the inspiring story of Carol Ray.

A couple of years ago Carol was about to complete a very successful career in the corporate world and retire to a very quiet life in a motor home, away from everything. She and her now adult children had struggled with various health challenges, and now that work life was completing, she just wanted to escape from it all.

Then, one morning, she had a dream with these very clear words, "Heal yourself and heal the world." Carol didn't know exactly what it meant but was so motivated by it that - as the very practical person she is - she created a PowerPoint presentation, in 10 languages, asking people to pray and meditate, in unison, for healing. Soon after, her new friend Sara Morell sent her a link to a page with an invitation by me to join a Miracle Experiment involving principles from the book Ancient Secrets of a Master Healer. The tagline on the page matched the exact words that had come to her in the dream:

"Heal yourself and heal the world."

She applied to become a volunteer and immediately began both helping herself and others. Along the way by reading the book, joining the free Sunday Global Healing calls, experiencing the courses created from it all she found not only physical, but also mental and emotional healing. She also found a fulfilling purpose, secrets leading to deep healing for some of her immediate family, and a new global family based on love.

Through it all, she also discovered something so profound and enjoyable in the Ancient Secrets of a Master Healer...

What if healing can be delicious?

You'll read more of her story on the upcoming pages, about how it was love for her son that initially inspired her desire to create this cookbook - with recipes that followed the Ancient Secrets she was learning. She wanted something that could help people who don't cook often, like her son, to have at their fingertips easy recipes that create healthy and delicious food.

To help in this mission, Carol invited the Ancient Secrets Community to get involved - and they have been awesome! Many have contributed recipes (from around the world), and others have been helping test recipe by recipe... to ensure it leads to easy, tasty, delicious, healing food.

Carol and her team also compiled additional resources so you can better understand which food is a medicine versus a poison for you. This - according to the Ancient Secrets of Siddha-Veda and Ayurveda - depends on your unique body type... and the resources in this book can give you more clarity on what is best for you!

Seeing all the love this team put into creating this book truly inspires me. I'm also inspired by how they wanted the proceeds to go to the Ancient Secrets Foundation to support our orphan kids in Nepal and other charitable causes.

Combining powerful ancient secrets with love... and you can change your life forever. We also call it 'Contagious Healing' because as you do this yourself, automatically it will begin to bless the lives of others you love.

I'm so excited that love guided you here, now.

I'm also eager to see what happens next as you experience how delicious it is to eat food that truly nourishes your body, mind, and emotions.

What magical things can happen in your life as love guides you?

Much love and respect,
Dr. Clint G. Rogers

Siddha-Veda Practitioner & Author of 'Ancient Secrets of a Master Healer'

P.S. We want to make sure you have these additional resources that can support you on your journey:

- Free mailing list
- Free Sunday Global Healing Miracle calls
- Appointments with a Practitioner who can customize the Ancient Secrets to You
- Life-Changing Training/Courses options
- Guided Delicious Detox options
- Free website for cookbook updates and recipe sharing: www.MyAncientSecrets.com/recipes

- Cookbook YouTube Channel: www.youtube.com/@AncientSecretsCookbook
- Ancient Secrets for Kids
- Ancient Secrets for Pets
- *Ancient Secrets of a Master Healer: A Western Skeptic, An Eastern Master, And Life's Greatest Secret*s (being translated & published in 30+ languages)
- Volunteer opportunities on the Miracle Dream Team

P.S.S. Big THANK YOU to Carol and each of you... as proceeds from this book go to support orphans, homeless, and other humanitarian projects through Ancient Secrets Foundation.

In fulfillment of Carol's dream, while you are healing yourself, through food, it is also helping to heal the world.

For more information, comments, questions, or inquiry:

Team@MyAncientSecrets.com

Dipo Bhakshayate Dhyant – Wir sind was wir essen!

A lamp eats darkness by providing light in the night. In the process, it produces soot or ash. Like the light, we are what we eat. Even if we do good for humanity, eating wrong food will destroy us.

Ayushakti's mission is to bring real health in every home by sharing knowledge, ancient wisdom, helping people using 6 breakthrough tools of Diet, Kitchen Remedies, Herbal Formulas, Lifestyle, Marmaa points, and Detox. By helping to create this book, Carol is contributing to people's lives in the most practical manner. This small book will provide tools to follow the diet and lifestyle which will create remarkable transformation in people's life. Big Salute and Gratitude to Carol Ray for putting together such powerful content. Lots of love to Carol.

I am with you, and I love you!

- Dr. Smita Naram

Note from the Author:

"Let thy medicine be food – let food be thy medicine."

Who doesn't want vibrant health? Most people have no idea where to start. Food was always more of a poison than medicine for me and my family. We didn't have genetic information at the time, but I would eventually understand that we carry a genetic disorder called Ehlors-Danlos. It explains why my mother's intestines ruptured after taking antibiotics and why she had to have a colostomy in her mid-forties. That alone is great motivation to better understand my body's relationship with food. My youngest son was diagnosed with celiac disease in the late seventies, and I spent days at the college library trying to understand how to feed him. Gluten-free has been an on-going learning process for years!

I discovered Dr. Naram's diet and lifestyle modifications about the time we all discovered COVID-19. It has been a game-changer! 75-90% reduction in pain! I wanted to create a cookbook that family, friends, and everyone else could use to make delicious food that would change their relationship with food forever!

My hope is that it will inspire you to try new and different ways of fueling your body for optimum, vibrant health, unlimited energy, and peace of mind. Take your time; listen to your body when it tells you it needs something. If you indulge in things 'not good for you,' try and enjoy them to the maximum extent, then do better tomorrow.

It will be helpful if you know your body type, called a 'Dosha' in Siddha-Veda. Knowing your Dosha helps to identify what is medicine for you and what is poison. My Dosha Quiz is included on page 209.

My sincere appreciation to Dr. Clint G. Rogers for this opportunity, to Dr. Smita Naram and the entire Ayushakti team, and to everyone in the Ancient Secrets Community who helped bring this vision to life!

I love you and I am with you.
Carol Ray, M.Ed., Texas, USA
Volunteer

Contents

Master Jivaka

Master Jivaka said everything can be either a
poison or a medicine, depending on how
it is used.

The same can be said for the food we eat.
What provides nourishment
for one might cause suffering for another.

The recipes here are based on Ancient Secrets
guidelines from Dr. Pankaj Naram, Siddha-Veda
practitioners, Ayushakti Ayurveda practitioners, and
the author's own research and experience.

For a personalized, individualized diet specifically
for your health and wellbeing, you are highly
encouraged to consult with a trained practitioner.

For more recipes beyond this book and videos on how to make many of the recipes here, please visit our recipe sharing site: www.MyAncientSecrets. com/recipes

You can request to host a pulse clinic, and/or get on the waiting list for a pulse consultation by Dr. Clint G. Rogers or another trained practitioner by going here: www.MyAncientSecrets.com/consultations

Either will guide you forward to the correct dietary recommendations, and potentially herbs, for your specific body type. To live with vibrant health is the greatest accomplishment in life.

Without a healthy body, a sound mind and emotional tranquility, all other aspects of our lives will be negatively impacted. Our intention for sharing with you the gift of Siddha-Veda lifestyle is only to empower you, and not to limit you.

To become independent and free of disease one needs inspiration, guidance, and an understanding of how our body responds to certain foods, lack of sleep, our environment, relationships, social life, too much or too little physical activities, work schedule, and so on.

Discover 'Ancient Secrets of a Master Healer: A Western Skeptic, An Eastern Master, And Life's Greatest Lessons.' https://www.MyAncientSecrets.com

Success Stories from Around the World

For me just getting the Pitta down in 3 generations has changed my life. Also, I don't see my scalp anymore and my hair is getting thicker.

I am happier and I have found another way to serve through cooking healthy for others and myself: a new modality and social skill. My belly never hurts anymore. I feel Blessed!

Dr. Ann Wilkinson, Osteopathic Bodywork
AmogaLife.com

Prior to learning the ancient secrets, I was experiencing a lot of bloating, constipation, and breakouts in my skin. After having a pulse consultation with Dr. Clint G. Rogers, I learned that raw leafy greens are not good for my body as well as dairy and

gluten. I not only eliminated these but also became a vegetarian. The results were more energy, better sleep, normalized stool, and clear skin. Another amazing 'side-effect' is a clearer and calmer mind.

I am so grateful that the ancient secrets taught me how to change my lifestyle and diet and that I now can help others with this knowledge.
- *Monica Posada*

"Before Ancient Secrets I was eating so clean… no dairy, no wheat, no refined sugar, and hardly any meat. For over 10 years, every day I'd eaten a green smoothie in the morning, and a large quantity of raw salad and vegetables during the day. I was also balancing my diet with a  mixture of grains and nuts. I'd done everything I had been taught that was a healthy, balanced diet.

However, I found myself still having low energy and pain in my body. After having my pulse consultation with Dr. Clint G. Rogers, I learned that based on my Doshas, raw food was not good for me. So I changed, I eliminated the raw salads and smoothies. I ensured I still had the same amount of vegetables I was consuming before but instead of raw I would lightly cook them. After a month of my new diet, I started to notice significantly more energy.

My digestive power started to increase, and my body began absorbing the nutrients better. Since then, I've helped many of my friends and family, who've benefited so much, too. Through the Ancient Secrets, I now understand better what is best for me and my body."
- *Punam Patel, www.punampatelhypnotherapy.com*

Myalgic Encephalomyelitis/CFS is usually a life sentence in the Western Medicine world. By the time I met Dr. Clint in February 2021, my life was limited to being horizontal, either on the couch or, on very bad days, the bed. If I went out it was

for medical appointments in a wheelchair, due to profound fatigue and days, weeks, or months of severe repercussions if I exceeded my "energy envelope." Constant all over body pain, headaches, frequent sore throats, debilitating brain fog, and a myriad of other symptoms were my normal. The physical, mental, and emotional challenges were devastating for me and my family.

By grace, friends told us about Dr. Clint and his book, and I was able to have a pulse consultation with him. I changed my diet and used the herbal formulas he recommended for me. Within seven months I was hiking, with no post-exertional consequences! I told Dr. Clint I feel like I am living a miracle! Nothing can describe the joy of being able to participate in life again in ways I thought were lost forever. As it says in the book, "If you change your food, you can change your future."

-       *Katie Amodio, MS. Waldorf Extra Lesson Teacher*

My mom told me about Dr. Naram and Dr. Clint.

I ended up having an online session with Dr. Meera who prescribed me a specific diet and supplements.

After 3 months of using the supplements, many of my symptoms improved. I then did the Healthiime Detox™. Most of my symptoms disappeared. The Pitta (heat) in my body reduced significantly. I am 80% better!!! I don't have any hives, burning rashes, pain in my abdomen, swollen ankles, etc.

Woo hoo!! I can hug someone wearing perfume with ease in my mind!! (No allergic reactions!)

Although I still now and then get some pain in my shoulder and wrist, I am able to do illustrations and design work as long as I pace myself and take regular breaks. I can go for a light jog and do very gentle yoga! I feel calmer and more peaceful in myself.

I feel so blessed and thankful to God to be alive and well, and thankful to Dr. Naram and the Siddha-Veda lineage for the healing dietaryrecommendations, home recipes, and supplements.

I am incredibly grateful to learn about Ayurveda from Dr. Meera, Dr. Hemang, Dr. Komal and the Ayushakti team.
– *Maryam Khalifah Maryamart.illustration@gmail. com*

I eat simply. Fresh from the farm to taste their true flavors. Lots of vegetables, few fruits, almost no grains. Four times a year I fast in moong and vegetables for 7-10 days. Occasionally, I eat what is offered no matter what. Until my 20's, I was dull, overweight, stuttering, 'slothy.' I radically changed my diet and lifestyle at 21. Ayurvedic change at 31. Eat fresh, spiced well, warm, and nutritious food. Now I live simply so others may simply live. At 58 I am pain free and full of energy. – *Dr. Stephen Wechsler* *NetworkHealingArts@gmail. com*

All in all, it was a learning curve, meaning the detox and the adventure of doing it, with its challenges and benefits.

Being on the correct side of a healthy lifestyle is worth the challenge; and experiencing the positive effect of meeting like-minded people in the support groups and Dr. Clint's Sunday zoom meetings have been life-changing. I am not free of symptoms but knowing that I am not alone and having a large global family around me the same path is great.

-*Arati Malavalli-Majd, MD*

You know that old saying, 'You don't know, what you don't know,' applies to me. I thought I felt pretty good. I'm sure a part of me knew I needed to change my diet, and certainly my sugar intake!

Eating moong bean soup is not only delicious, but it also gave me a new sense of confidence and balance I have never had before and the bonus, I lost weight (over 35 lbs.) without even trying.

My cravings disappeared and were replaced with a sense of well-being and peace that is profound. Nature does provide us with everything!

- *Ronney Aden*

Since I learned about Moong Bean Soup and how to make it, I have fallen in love with it. It has been a food staple in my life, where I have it for lunch usually 5 days a week. I can feel my body  loving it. Also, I take pure Ghee every day, which I know is balancing my Doshas. I am also now gluten-free, dairy-free, and nightshades-free. As a result, I feel that I have much more energy in my body.

Also, since eating moong bean soup almost every day and detox tea, I am never constipated anymore. I have also learned so many home remedies and Marmaas that have made such a difference in my life like feeling a cold or something coming on and then feeling much better a couple of hours after drinking the Immunity tea. I have been enjoying much better sleep with all that I am doing with food, home remedies, and Marmaas.
- *Luke Sutton*

I had many food sensitivities in the past. I was dealing with acid reflux and joint pain. I have been Gluten-free and Dairy-free for the last 5 years. After joining the Ancient Secrets, I came to know I need to make some changes in my diet like no sour food, no raw food, according to my constitution and low Agni.

I did my 28 days detox. I have added more moong beans, vegetables, and Ghee to my diet. I got creative to make more moong bean recipes to add to my everyday meal. Now I have more energy, more mental clarity, and no joint pain.

It's been a blessing to be part of the Ancient Secrets Community.
— *Keerty Das, Chef & Food Business Entrepreneur*

By changing the way that I eat to the new way as demonstrated in this beautiful cookbook, my acid reflux, migraines, gallbladder issues, and high blood pressure are now all manageable.

Additionally, I released 30 pounds and have managed to keep it off. Even my muscles are stronger! When I eat moong bean soup, I get an overall sense of well-being and when I eat according to guidance of Dr. Naram, I am stronger, healthier, & happier.

- Jayna C. Taylor

https://www.facebook.com/jayna.c.taylor?mibex tid=LQQJ4d

I am vegetarian and always thought that my diet is very good. With Ancient Secrets I learned about the diet for my body constitution, and my health has improved.

Moreover, I learned simple ways of improving and maintaining my health and found the world's best community. It is always an adventure to try out new recipes and share it with friends and family.

Happy cooking.

- *Aparna Yardi, Sr. Software Engineer*

My path of natural healing has been ongoing for many years. It has always been my natural inclination, although when I was in my twenties and burning the candle at both ends...working until 2 am, then hanging out after with friends drinking wine and smoking and eating whatever I felt like. At least I was working out, right?! Well, it caught up to me in my thirties when I heard the doctor utter the words we all fear, "You have cancer." I was diagnosed with stage 4 lymphoma (blood cancer).

My life flashed before me, along with flashes of the life I hadn't had a chance to live yet. The child I didn't have the chance to have. When I was able to accept and allow the possibility that I may not live, my feelings turned to the things I could do to help myself, and natural healing modalities I knew of. It takes years for the body to break down, and it takes time to detoxify and rebuild. I began the process of learning more and more about all the different gentle, natural, and effective solutions there are for health and healing and began feeling better.

- *Jody Curtis* http://www.jodycurtis.com/

I love food. I was an emotional eater and although 'healthy' in my choices, my weight fluctuated and crept up well above what was healthy for me. Over the course of many years, I began having nerve twitching in my legs and pain in my feet. I got to a place where I knew something had to change and quickly. A dear friend gave me Dr. Clint's book and it spoke to my heart and soul.

I immediately completely altered my diet following the principles recommended and in 9 months lost 24lbs. I no longer eat my emotions. I began herbs and did several detoxes eradicating the nerve pain 90% and eliminating all pain in my feet.

My heart has opened to new vistas and my energy is steady and consistent. This cookbook is a gift to create healthy, healing, loving food for mind/body/soul.

-        *Susan Minden Engman, PhD; Psychologist*

Despite eating a healthy diet, staying active and fit, years of body stress and traumas led to degenerative changes in some of my joints and the inflammation was painful. Ibuprofen™ had become a daily practice like vitamins. After the 28-day detox and the herbs, I no longer needed or took anti-inflammatories. I eliminated foods and became more conscious of lifestyle and harmony with my body. Digestion and how I feel after eating is more important than what I eat.

Change your diet, change your life!

-Joseph E. Engman, D.O.; Orthopedic Surgeon

Six Instruments of Siddha-Veda

According to the philosophy and the ancient teachings of Siddha-Veda, there are six essential instruments necessary to achieve a lasting and vibrant health. These include:

- Diet
- Lifestyle
- Herbal Formulas
- Marmaa
- Ashtakarma/Panchakarma
- Home Remedies

These six instruments act like pillars that hold and support the well-being of your physical, mental, and emotional body. To create and maintain balance and harmony in your life, the ancient art and science of Siddha-Veda offers simple and precise guidelines.

At first the lifestyle and the diet may seem restrictive and at times impossible to follow. With modern life's busy schedules and so many distractions it is no surprise that many people gravitate towards recipes that are familiar, many ingredients which are easily available, ready-made food loaded with additives, preservatives, and fillers, and so on. Some people may also think that eating healthily is less convenient and more expensive.

This may be true in the short term, but in the long run, by continuing to consume the kinds of toxic foods and gigantic portions, we are all paying a heavy price that can no longer be ignored.

Also, the occurrence of so many preventable diseases such as

- Type 2 Diabetes
- Obesity
- Hypertension
- High cholesterol
- ADD and ADHD

and many more...should be a wake-up call to everyone in our society.

The subject of food is not only a cultural part of everyone's upbringing but also a highly emotional aspect of our lives. Whether it is the process of purchasing the ingredients, or preparing the food, or simply remembering the tastes and the aromas associated with memories of holidays and sitting around with family and friends, these memories shape the very foundation of our approach to health and lifestyle as well as influence the choices we make daily.

Also, our environment plays a very important role in the choices we make. The food trends in the supermarket emphasized through media and the press sway us in a certain direction. This flood of information affects our belief system and creates different emotions in connection to food and overall well-being.

Bad Gut Bacteria is linked to Depression

Recent research studies have determined links between our emotional state and the state of our gut bacteria. One reason Dr. Naram's diet is so effective is that after eating healthily for only 4-5 days, most people can start to see improvement in their mood! Why is this?

Animal models strongly suggest gut bacteria (also called microbiome) play an important role in anxiety and trauma-related disorders. Transplanting bad bacteria from a depressed mouse to a healthy mouse created depression in the previously healthy mouse. And taking healthy gut bacteria from the healthy mouse to the depressed mouse improved the depressed mouse's mental health. The good news is you don't have to have a bacteria transplant to lift your depression! Just try this new approach to eating and discover if you can break the dependency you have on foods that cause discomfort, anxiety, or depression.

For additional information:
-The Gut Microbiome and Mental Health: Implications for Anxiety- and Trauma-Related Disorders - PubMed (nih.gov)

When you hear that still, small voice inside saying you need SUGAR, or a soda, or cake or cookies, ask if the request is coming from your GUT or your BRAIN. Chances are, when you start limiting your sugar intake, your cravings will lessen and may even go away at some point! Have a fig, date, apple, or similar, and see if you can get through the craving without caving!

"Create strong digestion and improve your immunity using powerful ancient Siddha-Veda Principles to change your life forever."

~ Master Baba Ramdas

As told to Dr. Pankaj Naram

Research is showing that therapeutic herbs, used for thousands of years in Siddha-Veda and Ayurveda, have healing properties that create a prebiotic effect and increase the beneficial microbes in our guts. At the same time, it looks like they are also reducing the number of harmful bacteria. These are the same bad gut bacteria that hijack the neurotransmitters to the brain and create cravings.

These new findings on the power of herbs - providing both prebiotic and post-biotic health-promoting capabilities - give us a better understanding of how our digestive system works and its connection to depression or well-being.

Starving the bad bacteria by withholding refined sugar and adding these powerful herbs can reduce your pain and inflammation over time and give you more of a sense of peace and calm.

Recommendations on Where to Start

The goal of this cookbook is to help you create healthy digestion and a strong immune system. Even if you can follow only one or two of the recommendations at first, you will find that over time you can incorporate more changes. It is important to be consistent, but please remember to enjoy your food, enjoy your life. Get out in nature and learn to stop and just 'be.' Breathe.

Express gratitude every day!

Where to start?

One place to start is to determine your Dosha, (see Dosha Quiz on page 184) to help you determine your current imbalance. Select the foods that will help you get back in balance. Starting with a 7-Day Detox can help rid your body of bad bacteria that are smart enough to convince you that you must have sugar! Once they start dying off, due to a lack of sugar, it gets so much easier!

Maybe adding a teaspoon of Ghee to your morning will be just the boost you need to improve your digestion, the texture of your skin, your arteries, and more! Or try the *Energy Power Breakfast* on page 38 to get that extra kick you have been missing in the morning.

Use the Forgive and Forget Marmaa (left- hand, soft tissue between the thumb and index finger: press 6 times and work up to six times daily). It will help you move on and maybe tomorrow will be better! And when you have a good day, are loving yourself and others, pat your heart six times with your right hand and say, "Well done, Me!"

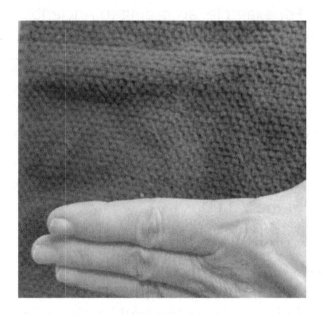

Vitamins and Minerals

Many times, people are in a complete panic and are expressing fear about recent vitamin levels in blood work or some form of mineral deficiencies or toxicities. Let us look at the subject of vitamins and minerals from the point of view of Dr. Pankaj Naram's Siddha-Veda lineage. In the ancient teachings of Siddha-Veda, the emphasis is on complete and proper digestion of food and the prevention of toxic accumulations (Aam) not on the amount of vitamins and minerals present in the food. A correct and complete digestive process in turn guarantees the balance in the body's Doshas (constitution).

Every food has its own characteristics and attributes. For example, according to Ancient Siddha-Veda Principles, milk and dairy products' attributes are heavy, cold, and mucus-producing, or we can say that they create an imbalance of the Kapha Dosha. Fermented and sour foods have the acidic characteristic, and therefore they create an imbalance of the Pitta Dosha. Dry and raw foods have inflammatory attributes and create an imbalance of the Vata Dosha.

In other words, the purpose of eating is that the attributes of the food must help to balance the Doshas: Vata, Pitta, and Kapha, and not add to the toxins accumulated in the body in the form of undigested food. Vitamin or mineral contents of the food can only benefit the body if the food is fully digested, metabolized, and the elimination process is regular and successful.

What Do You Want?

Do you want to have less pain in your belly? A slimmer waistline? Better night's sleep? Or just be the best version of you that you can be?

One of the most important ancient secrets can help you discover what you want. What do you want --- from your body, from your mind, from your emotions, from your life? What if you don't know what you want?

Dr. Naram's Marmaa Shakti Secret for Discovering What You Want: (*Ancient Secrets of a Master Healer* p.136)

1. Close your eyes and imagine a white frame in front of your right eye.

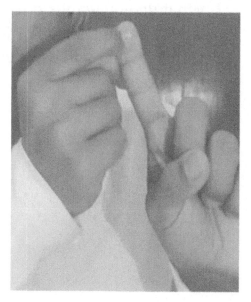

2. On your right-hand pointer (index) finger, press the top portion 6 times, with your thumb and index finger of your left hand and ask yourself, "What do I want?"

3. When you get an answer, write it down in your journal, then pat your heart 6 times and say, "Well done! Good job!"

4. Continue to use the same process and ask what you want specifically for your body. Be sure and determine what you WANT, and not what you don't want, which is our natural tendency.

5. What do you want for your mind? To be more calm and peaceful or more energetic and creative? This same marmaa can help with that as well.

6. How are your emotions? Up and down, flat, erratic, muted, or something else? Do you tell yourself, "I feel tired" then yawn? Being tired is an emotion. What do you want from your emotions?

7. What do you want from your life? More creativity, more stability? More flexibility? Determine what you want using the marmaa and write it down.

Dr. Pankaj Naram

If thy food is:
FROZEN
CANNED
PROCESSED
DEAD

It maketh YOU feel:
FROZEN
CANNED
PROCESSED
DEAD

~ Dr. Pankaj Naram

Basic Terms

Aam: Aam is the name given to the physical toxins in the body which are produced due to undigested food, ingested pollutants, or emotionally and mentally stressful experiences. Excess Aam leads to our bodily systems being clogged or blocked, because it is not excreted by our natural systems. It leads to fermentation and subsequent imbalance in all three Doshas. Aam (toxic material) is the fertile ground for the development of disease. It has no useful function within the body, it is only destructive and is best avoided and removed.

Agni: Agni (enzymes and hormones) is the metabolic or digestive fire. It helps digest whatever we eat and converts it into nutritional plasma and feces. The lymph and blood stream absorb the nutritional plasma and transform it into various tissues (Dhatus) with the aid of Dhatu Agni (metabolic fire or metabolic enzymes). As every bodily function is based on transformation, which in turn is supported by Agni, if Agni is diminished, then so are all our bodily functions.

Dhatus: There are seven types of Dhatus (tissues) in the body, which are plasma, blood, muscle, fat, bone, bone marrow, and reproductive fluid.

Doshas: are predominantly made of 5 elements: earth, water, fire, air, and space (ether). Siddha-Veda suggests that these Doshas, Kapha, Vata, and Pitta, are the primary qualities or principles that govern every human body.

- **Kapha:** Composed of water and earth, Kapha is responsible for structure of the body, rejuvenation, stability, energy and maintaining immunity. When imbalanced, it creates lethargy, overgrowth, blockages, and mucus. For example, heart disease is associated with congestion in the arteries.

- **Pitta:** is composed of fire and water. It is responsible for digestion, metabolism, absorption, transformation and governing of body temperature. When imbalanced, it creates excessive anger, frustration, irritation, skin problems, acidity, and inflammatory disorders in the body.

- **Vata:** is composed of air and space. It is responsible for every mental, emotional, and physical movement, including urination, bowel and intracellular movements, joint and muscle movements, thought processes, blood, air and food movements, just to name a few. When imbalanced, Vata disturbs the movement and creates tremors, stiffness in the joints and pain, anxiety, fear, insomnia, lack of energy, degeneration, overactive mind, and lack of concentration.

Srotas: are physical channels within the body, from large ones like the digestive tract, to the microscopic ones at a cellular level. Srotas carry blood, sweat, pancreatic fluid, semen, and feces, and this is how nutrients reach our cells, as well as how we excrete waste. To keep these channels open and flexible is, of course, essential to having good health.

Gunas: are groupings of different qualities of energy, which are Sattva (goodness, purity, light), Rajas (energy, passion, birth), and Tamas (darkness, destruction, death). They define and reflect our health, behavior, thinking, and diet.

Ojas: is the residual pure energy that is vital for maintaining our body's immune system. It is generated at the end of the conversion process. Healthy tissues (Dhatus) and immunity (Ojas) promote positive emotions, immunity, vitality, strength, health, anti-aging, fast recovery from chronic problems, enthusiasm, and tranquility of the mind.

Understanding of Bodily Functions

Dr. Pankaj Naram believed that every illness starts with weak digestion and metabolism (low Agni). This creates Aam (toxins) and excess Dosha (imbalance). Excess Dosha and Aam block channels and bodily functions. Finally, tissues become undernourished, and illness is created.

The key is to create transformation using the six tools of Siddha-Veda – i.e., diet, home remedies, lifestyle changes, Panchakarma (detoxification), herbal formulas, and Marmaa Shakti to shift imbalances at the root. This holistic approach amazingly supports the entire system to bring back long-lasting health naturally.

Guidelines for a Healthy Lifestyle

Siddha-Veda suggests that food is medicine.

Food is a source of life, and digestion is the basis of health. A primary sign of good health is that your Agni is working well, which is the prerequisite for digesting the food you are eating efficiently. This will ensure that all the necessary nutrients are distributed into every cell, and at the same time, that all waste products are burned off completely without leaving any deposits of toxins in the body.

In Siddha-Veda, no good or bad foods exist, only food that is good or bad for YOU. Whether a food is good or bad for you depends on your constitution, or, more specifically, which Dosha(s) is (are) predominant in your body.

This approach to eating is focused on Dosha balancing, Aam reduction, increasing Agni, and nourishing the tissues (Dhatus) and immune system. As there are many variables as to how to balance the Doshas, particularly when imbalances have manifested in the form of an illness or certain symptoms, we recommend that you follow the recommendations of a trained practitioner of the Ancient Secrets, rather than just following a Dosha balancing diet.

Changing One's Habits

Changing how we eat takes time. Our food habits are quite central to our sense of self - socially, culturally, and historically. Getting started takes some courage and commitment, as mental and emotional energy must be engaged.

In the beginning, effort may be required to find new recipes and experiment with purchasing, cooking, and eating foods that are unfamiliar.

When faster healing, better health, and improved quality of life are the rewards, these benefits give the energy and enthusiasm to go on. We experiment further, discover what does and does not work for us, and become confident enough to share some of our new-found recipes with family and friends.

How you eat is as important as what you eat, because the quality of digestion (Agni) is affected by the condition of your mind, emotions, and environment. To promote healing and good health, it's suggested that you:

- Eat at regular times - no snacking
- Eat only when hungry
- Eat slowly and chew the food well
- Do not overeat, just enough to feel pleasantly 'full'
- Take a short walk or lie on your left side for 10 minutes after eating to improve digestion.

In general, you are encouraged to eat:

- Fresh foods that are in season and locally grown
- Warm, soupy, fresh, cooked foods, rather than cold, stale, canned, raw, or dry foods
- Ghee (not clarified butter), herbs (basil, celery, etc.) and spices (garlic, ginger, cumin, cinnamon, cardamom, turmeric, black pepper, etc.) that aid digestion.

Vata and Pitta: Foods to avoid:

• Heavy-to-digest foods such as wheat, meat (especially red meat), and refined sugar. These foods severely decrease the digestive fire (Agni) and produce mucus and toxins (Aam).

• Deep-fried foods are also heavy to digest and highly Vata increasing. If meat is eaten at all, one should stick to white meat only, i.e., chicken and turkey.

• Fish is a heat inducing food and increases Pitta but can be enjoyed occasionally. If eaten, one should choose fresh-water fish rather than seafood.

• Sour foods such as tomatoes, all sour fruits (oranges, pineapples, lemons, limes, grapefruits, etc.), vinegars, and hot spices like chilies. These foods increase Pitta and heat in the body as well as reduce the digestive power (especially tomatoes). Parsnips aggravate Vata and Pitta.

• Fermented or fermentation-increasing foods such as yogurt, alcohol, cheese (especially old and hard ones) and yeast- containing foods such as veggie pâtes, soy sauce, and beer. All fermented foods are sour in nature and therefore have Pitta increasing qualities. Whenever there is too much Pitta and heat in the intestines, fermentation is multiplied, thus resulting in gas and decreased digestive capacity.

• Ice-cold foods and drinks are immediate 'killers' for digestive fire. They are best avoided totally, but if taken, avoid directly before, after, or together with meals.

• Avoid ready-made, canned (tinned) and microwaved foods! They are devoid of real nutritional value, deplete the digestive fire, and produce toxins in the body.

If you have the Vata / Pitta constitution: eat more cooked vegetables, squashes and pumpkin, moong, moong dal (or dahl), lentils, and cooked green leafy vegetables. Avoid tomatoes, peppers (capsicum), eggplant (brinjal), ground nuts (peanuts), lemon, lime, grapefruit, chili, and pungent foods.

Kapha: Foods to Avoid:

• Heavy to digest foods such as wheat, meat (especially red meat) and refined sugar. These foods severely decrease the digestive fire (Agni) and produce mucus and toxins (Aam).

• Deep fried foods are also heavy to digest and highly Vata and Kapha increasing.

• Sour foods such as tomatoes, all sour fruits (oranges, pineapples, grapefruits etc.), and vinegars increase Kapha and irritation in the throat and increase Aam.

- Fermented or fermentation-increasing foods such as yogurt, alcohol, hard cheese, and yeast-containing foods such as Marmite, soy sauce, and beer. All fermented foods are sour in nature and therefore have Kapha and Pitta increasing qualities.

- Raw vegetables, sprouted beans, and leafy green salads are hard to digest, cooling, and Kapha/Vata producing. Broad, black-eyed, and kidney beans, chickpeas, kohlrabi, Brussels sprouts, and cabbage should be avoided even when cooked for most people.

- Ice-cold foods and drinks are immediate 'killers' for the digestive fire and are highly Kapha increasing.

- Avoid ready-made, tinned, and microwaved foods! They are devoid of life force (Prana), deplete the digestive fire, and produce toxins in the body.

- Avoid all dairy products, milk, soy milk, and minimize all sweet fruits, avocado, bananas, berries, melon, grapes, peaches, pears, and plums.

If you have a Kapha constitution: eat more vegetable soups. Spice your foods with turmeric, black pepper, garlic, and asafetida (hing).

Breakfast Options

- Energy Power Breakfast - Dr. Naram
- Moong beans or Kitchari
- Steel-cut oatmeal or instant oatmeal with raisins or cranberries
- Porridge (use almond milk) with cinnamon and cardamom
- Scrambled eggs
- Vegetable omelet
- Gluten-free muffin
- Sweet fruits (steamed organic apples, pears, peaches) with cloves
- Banana slices fried in Ghee with cinnamon and spices
- Protein and veggie-based shakes

Energy Power Breakfast

- Dr. Pankaj Naram

Ingredients:

- 4 small dates or 1 fig
- 2-4 blanched almonds
- 2 whole cardamom pods
- 1 tsp. fennel seeds
- ½ tsp. Ghee

Directions:

Soak all except Ghee overnight.

Drain and peel cardamom and almonds. Add half glass water and Ghee. Blend mixture and drink or chew everything until it turns into a liquid.

***This breakfast will keep your energy high throughout the day. The dates and almonds provide energy and nutrients full of iron, potassium, protein, and B vitamins. The fennel and cardamom increase digestive energy. Have breakfast later only if you are really hungry.

Beetroot-Finger Millet Pancakes

- *Shilpi Gupta*

The background story... After my 100-day course and the 30-day detox, I've been very conscious of making healthy choices and always looking for ways of incorporating moong beans and all the healthy ingredients in my cooking. When I couldn't eat beetroots, I had to look for ways to incorporate it. The finger millet isabsolutely great. The best part is that my kids love these pancakes and what more could I ask for?

Take the moong bean pancake up a notch by adding beet roots and finger millet flour (Ragi flour).

Ingredients:

- 4 small peeled and boiled beets
- 1 cup presoaked moong bean
- 1 cup finger Millet (Ragi) flour
- Salt to taste
- Green chilies 2-3 or as per your tolerance
- Curry leaves 15-20
- 2 tsp. cumin seeds
- Ghee, avocado, or coconut oil

Directions:

Blend everything to a consistency of a batter that can be easily spread on a pan. If it gets thick, add water slowly. If it is runny, add Ragi flour to get a desired consistency. Heat some Ghee, avocado, or coconut oil in a skillet or flat pan. Pour a spoonful on the pan, spread it with love. Cook for a few minutes on either side and enjoy it with family.

Cardamom Millet Porridge w Berry Compote

- Punam Patel

I love this recipe; it's warming and light but indulgent with berries and pistachios and a burst of cardamom. I was experimenting with leftover millet one day and it turned out great.

Ingredients:

- ½ cup millet
- 1 cup oat milk (or milk of preference)
- ½ cup blueberries/ strawberries
- ½ teaspoon ground cardamom
- 1 tablespoon maple syrup
- ½ teaspoon of vanilla
- Pinch of salt
- 5-6 pistachio nuts chopped

Directions:

1. Cook the millet by adding 1 cup of water to boil and then simmer covered for 15 minutes or so.

2. In a separate pot add the berries, maple, vanilla & heat

3. Once the millet is cooked add the milk and heat on medium heat. Add a pinch of salt and the cardamom and keep stirring

4. Transfer the millet mixture to a bowl, pour the berry compote on top and sprinkle on the chopped pistachios.

5. Add more sweetener such as a drizzle of honey to taste if you prefer it sweeter.

Pan Cake

- Ken Wolkoff @2023 Ken Wolkoff

Ingredients:

- 1 cup barley flour
- 1 cup mixture of rice, oats, and barley with your choice of nuts like almonds, pecans, or macadamia nuts

- ½ tsp. cinnamon
- ¼ tsp. nutmeg
- ¼ tsp. cardamom
- 40 drops of vanilla extract
- ¼ tsp. salt
- 1 Tbsp. baking powder
- Sweetener (maple syrup, jaggery, and/or Stevia, etc.)
- (optional) Arrowroot, tapioca, or chia for some moisture and consistency
- ½ cup of blueberries, cherries, strawberries, raspberries, bananas, apples, etc. Can also add coconut flakes or chocolate chips.
- ½ cup of raisins
- Coconut oil to grease the pan (very small amount)

- 8 ounces coconut milk (1 whole coconut with meat blended to cream or 1 small can of organic coconut milk)
- Water to be added as needed

Directions:

This creation started with the love of blueberry buckwheat pancakes. One day instead of tediously flipping batches of pancakes, I decided to pour the whole bowl of batter into the large glass skillet I was using. I cooked the bottom lightly on the stove top then put the whole skillet in the broiler to cook from the top down as flipping the whole thing was not possible. This was the birth of the Pan-Cake which overlapped muffins, cake and pancakes and was much easier to make and able to be cooked at a lower temperature. Many iterations and combinations followed and like most good basic recipes, there is room for much addition and creativity.

Mix all the dry ingredients. I make the basic flour mix by using whole grains in the Vitamix™ grain attachment. Put the fruits and raisins as well as the pieces of nuts, coconut flakes, chocolate chips, or whatever you choose in a mixing bowl. Pour in the coconut milk and stir thoroughly. Add water if needed. The consistency should be that of a medium batter that slowly flows out of the bowl. A wide range of consistencies is possible, and each has a slightly different cooking time and final consistency.

Coat the skillet with coconut oil (easily spread with a spatula) and pour in the batter. Tap or use a utensil or spatula to even out the batter. Cook on stove top until a few bubbles surface or a bit of steam is seen. Do not overcook.

A second cooking method uses a flat glass casserole dish. Coat with oil and pour in batter. Bake as if it is a cake. I use 275 degrees F for about an hour. Slower, lower temperature cooking gives a more consistent penetration of the batter and has the benefits of lower temperature nutritionally. Later it is possible to flip sections of the cake and cook the uncooked side particularly if it is too moist. If slow cooked long enough the cake can dry out significantly and be used more like cookies or bars. It's great served with butter and maple syrup like traditional pancakes or with whipped cream or ice cream (coconut is my favorite). The basic technique of this method can be used to make a savory dish with onions, garlic, vegetables or added beans or as curry or with Mexican spices.

Millie's Moong Bean Crepes

- Millie Rogers

Serve for breakfast with steamed/stewed apples & cinnamon!

Ingredients:

- ½ cup of soaked moong (overnight)
- 1 cup Almond Breeze almond milk
- 2 eggs
- 1 Tbsp. Ghee
- ⅛ tsp. salt

Directions:

Blend all the ingredients together. Spoon on pan (coated with Ghee).

Cook till little holes show, about 2 mins. Turn and cook 1 minute longer. Serve with apple sauce, strawberries, or other fruits, or a drizzle of honey. Or serve savory with vegetables.

Photo Credit: Judy Lamar

Moong Bean Crepes

- *Shilpi Gupta*

Ingredients:

- 1 cup moong beans (soaked overnight)
- 2 green chilies (optional)
- Salt to taste
- 1 tsp. cumin
- 1 tsp. ginger garlic paste (reduces gas)
- 10-15 curry leaves – fresh (I love the flavor)

Directions:

Use a bit of Ghee, extra virgin olive oil, or avocado oil or a skillet. Blend the ingredients together to a fine consistency and not too thick so when we spread it, it can move easily. Set the initial flame on medium high, and after spooning into the pan, create about a 5"-6" circle, using the back of the spoon or spatula and go around and around to create a circle.

Reduce the heat and let it cook for 2-3 minutes until it is completely brown (bubbles form on the top). Carefully use a spatula to turn it over. Press along the edges to ensure the uncooked batter gets spread out. Continue to cook on medium heat until fully cooked.

Scrambled Eggs

- Carol Ray

Serves 2 People
Start with the freshest eggs available - free range, cage free, organic, etc.

Ingredients:

- 4 large or 5 medium sized eggs, cracked into a deep bowl
- 4-5 teaspoons filtered cold water
- 1 tsp. Ghee
- 2 Tbsp. minced yellow or white onion
- 1 tsp. minced garlic
- 1 handful of fresh spinach (optional)
- Salt and pepper to taste

Directions:

In a skillet greased with ghee, melt the Ghee on medium heat. Add the onion, garlic, and spinach to the melted Ghee. Add the water to the bowl of cracked eggs and whisk until well blended.

Stir the egg mixture into the skillet with the Ghee, onion, and garlic. Use a spatula to gently turn the eggs to prevent over cooking. Serve warm.

Steamed Organic Apples

- Carol Ray

Start with an organic apple and cut it into quarters lengthwise. Add two whole cloves to each apple quarter and place in about a half cup of purified/ filtered water in a saucepan, cover with a lid, and cook for 8-10 minutes on medium to low heat. Remove the core and the cloves and if digestion is an issue or you are detoxing, scoop the pulp from the skin and eat only the pulp.

Delicious
Main Dishes

TRI-DOSHA
GOOD FOR EVERYONE

GLUTEN-FREE
DAIRY-FREE
REFINED SUGAR-FREE

Nutritional Value of Moong (Mung)

Here is a fun clip where Dr. Giovanni Brincivalli discusses research and health benefits of whole green moong beans. https://youtu.be/tpcZVFs_MiU

Name	Amount	% Daily Value
Calories	347 kcal	
Carbohydrate	62.6 g	23% DV
Fiber	16.3 g	58% DV
Sugars	6.6 g	
Fat	1.15 g	1% DV
Saturated	0.35 g	2% DV
Monounsaturated	0.16 g	
Polyunsaturated	0.38 g	
Omega-3	0.03 g	
Omega-6	0.36 g	
Protein	23.86 g	48% DV

https://fdc.nal.usda.gov/fdc-app.html#/food-details/174256/nutrients

Nutritional Value of Moong (Mung) Cooked

One cup (7 ounces or 202 grams) of boiled mung beans contains (reference):

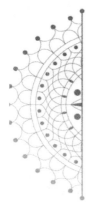 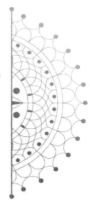

Calories: 212
Fat: 0.8 grams
Protein: 14.2 grams
Carbs: 38.7 grams
Fiber: 15.4 grams
Folate (B9): 80% of the Reference Daily Intake (RDI)
Manganese: 30% of the RDI
Magnesium: 24% of the RDI
Vitamin B1: 22% of the RDI
Phosphorus: 20% of the RDI
Iron: 16% of the RDI
Copper: 16% of the RDI
Potassium: 15% of the RDI
Zinc: 11% of the RDI
Vitamins B2, B3, B5, B6 and selenium

Moong Bean Soup Mastery

- Become a Master at Making Miraculous Moong Soup

- Helps to balance all three metabolic body types or Doshas: Vata, Pitta & Kapha.
- Aids the clearing away of Aam (toxicity) as a powerful detoxifier.
- Has anti-cancer and anti-inflammatory properties, helps diabetes, improves blood pressure levels and cholesterol, plus is very high in antioxidants, and is rich in vitamins and minerals.
- Best diet to speed up healing in the body (recommended with cooked green vegetables).
- One great benefit of eating only moong soup during a detox is that you are not eating all the other stuff that has been causing you problems.
- High in digestible protein - these beans are one of the best plant-based sources of protein. Rich in essential amino acids (amino acids that your body is unable to produce on its own), such as phenylalanine, leucine, isoleucine, valine, lysine, arginine, and more.
- High in soluble fiber and resistant starch, promoting and improving digestive health.

Magical Moong Bean Soup

- Millie Rogers, Utah, USA

Our family started eating moong bean soup after my husband, George, first returned from a 30-day cleanse in India.

George made the soup, and we probably ate it twice a week. After his passing, it came to me to make the soup.

I made sure I always had some available when Clint came home. It was after hearing about others' lack of pain that I decided to eat it with more regularity. It was after eating only moong soup for 2-1/2 days that I realized that the pain was gone in my knees when I was walking to a friend's house. I now eat it once or twice a day.

I recommend it to anyone who is in pain. - Millie Rogers (proud mother of Dr. Clint G. Rogers).

Ingredients:

- 1 cup moong beans soaked overnight – with 1 tsp. of baking soda. Rinse well.
- 2 Tbsp. Ghee over medium heat and add 1 tsp. black mustard seeds. Cook until seeds pop
- 1 heaping tbsp. minced garlic
- 1 Tbsp. powdered ginger

- 1 bay leaf
- 1 tsp. turmeric
- 1 tsp. coriander
- 1 tsp. cumin
- 1 tsp. garam masala
- 2 pinches of hing or asafetida
- 1 cup chopped onions
- 1 cup chopped carrots
- 2 stalks of chopped celery
- Add any other vegetable(s) you want
- 3 pieces of kokum chopped
- 7 cups of water
- 2-5 vegetable bouillon (or cubed chicken bouillon) or 2 tsp. Vegeta seasoning (the one without MSG)
- Add Lots of Love

Many of these ingredients may be purchased online (https://www. MyAncientSecrets.com/recipe)

Stovetop Directions:

1. Bring a large pot to heat, add the ghee, wait for it to melt.

2. Add mustard seeds and bay leaf, wait for mustard seeds to start popping.

3. Add turmeric, hing, cumin, coriander, garam masala and stir. If it starts to dry add a splash of water.

4. Add the garlic and ginger and mix well, cook for a minute. If it starts to dry add a splash of water.

5. Add salt and black pepper.

6. Add all the vegetables and diced kokum mix well, cook for a few minutes.

7. Meanwhile rinse the soaked moong to clean, then add it to the pot with the cooked spice mixture. Stir then add 7 cups of water.

8. Add the bouillon cube or vegetable stock powder.

9. Bring to a boil then turn the stove down to a simmer, cover with lid and cook for 50 minutes.

10. Once the moong is cooked, taste and add salt to preference. At this point you can also add more hot water if you want it more soupy in consistency. Add additional Ghee to your liking.

*Pressure Cooker/Instant Pot Directions:

1. Select the sauté option on your Instant Pot™ and then add the Ghee, wait for it to melt.

2. Follow steps 2-9 from above.

3. Select the "pressure cook" option, then manually select 10 minutes and "Start."

*If using a standard pressure cooker start by heating it on the stove then adding the Ghee. Follow steps 2-9. Pressure cook for 25 minutes or as per the instructions on your pressure cooker.

Kitchari

- *Carol Ray*

Ingredients:

- ½ cup Basmati rice (rinsed twice)
- ½ cup split moong beans (yellow moong dal) (rinsed twice)
- 1 Tbsp. Ghee (not clarified butter) or oil
- ½ tsp. black or brown mustard seeds
- ½ tsp. turmeric powder
- 1 pinch asafoetida (hing)
- ½ tsp. cumin powder
- ½ tsp. coriander
- 1 ½ tsp. fresh ginger, peeled & chopped
- ½ tsp. fresh garlic, peeled & chopped
- 1 cup of minced organic carrots
- 1 cup of minced onion
- 1 cup of cubed sweet potatoes
- 1 cup of minced organic celery
- 1-2 tsp. mineral salt or sea salt (adjust to taste)

Directions:

Put a tea kettle with 5 cups of water on medium high heat. In the meantime, heat the Ghee in a large deep saucepan, put in the spices and wait for the mustard seeds to pop. Sauté for a minute or so, then add the split moong beans and finally the rice. Stir until all foods are flavored and colored with the spice mixture. Add 4 cups of boiling water and let the food come to a boil. After 5 minutes, reduce heat to simmer and let it cook for about 30-35 minutes or until the beans are completely soft. Add a little salt.

You can add more water if you like a soupier consistency. Try different vegetables and spices to create variety. You can add your choice of vegetables during the last 10-15 minutes of cooking time. *These quantities can be doubled or modified for more flavor or different properties.

Moong Beans Handvo

- Arati Malavalli-Majd

(Vegan Burger Alternative) Moong beans Handvo, vegan modified original Gujarati recipe by Tarla Dalal, a famous Padma Shri decorated Indian female chef.

Cooking time: 2 hours 55 minutes; 2 servings.

Ingredients:

- ¼ cup full green moong bean
- ¼ cup yellow dal moong bean
- ¼ cup of water plus 1 extra tsp.
- 1 tablespoon gluten-free flour
- 1 ½ teaspoon besan (chickpea) flour
- 1 Tbsp. finely chopped coriander
- ½ cup mixed vegetables (carrots, green peas, French green beans, etc.) chopped and boiled
- 2-3 Tbsp. finely chopped onions
- Pinch black pepper
- Dash of turmeric
- 2 Tbsp. Ghee
- 1 tsp. mustard seeds
- 1 tsp. sesame seeds
- ¼ tsp. asafetida (hing)
- 1 tsp. fruit salt/baking soda

Directions:

- Soak both green and yellow moong beans together overnight, then drain and grind/mix them together with ¼ cup of water and mix well.

- Transfer to a deep bowl and add the spices and herbs except mustard and sesame seeds (they are added before cooking, as well as baking soda/fruit salt at end), and blend into a paste. Add ½ cup mixed veggies and 2-3 tablespoons of onion, finely chopped, black pepper, and dash of turmeric. Add the fruit salt and 1 tsp. of water evenly over the mixture and mix gently. Heat half of the Ghee in a 12.5 cm, (5") pan and add mustard seeds, sesame seeds, and Asafoetida, sauté on a medium flame for a few seconds.

- Pour ½ of the batter over it and spread evenly. Cover with a lid and cook on a medium flame for 10 minutes or until the base turns golden brown in color and crisp. Lift the Handvo gently using 2 large flat spoons and turn it over to the other side.

- Cover and cook for another 7-8 minutes or until it turns golden brown in color. Cool slightly and cut into equal pieces. Repeat for the second Handvo. Serve with any homemade dip of your liking.

Source:

- Adapted from https:// www.tarladalal.com/ green-moong-dal-handvo-40125r

White Zucchini-Basil Soup

- *Ronney Aden*

Ingredients:

- 500 g (about a pound) white- skinned, organic zucchini
- 1 handful fresh basil leaves, organic
- 1 small onion, organic
- 1 clove garlic, organic
- ½ tsp. turmeric powder, organic
- ½ tsp. cumin powder, organic
- ½ tsp. coriander powder, organic
- 1 pinch Asafoetida (hing)
- ½ tsp. black salt - according to taste
- 1 tsp. Ghee, organic

Directions:

1. Wash & cut zucchini into 1/2-inch pieces
2. Wash basil leaves
3. Heat 1 tsp. of Ghee in a pot
4. Add chopped onion and garlic
5. Add all spices and stir
6. Add chopped zucchini & sauté for 1 to 2 min.

7. Cover with hot water, bring to boil for 7 min.

8. Add basil leaves (set some aside for garnish)

9. Mix ready soup in a blender

10. Add salt to taste

11. Serve and garnish with some basil leaves

Thai Vegetable Curry

- Dr. Smita Naram

Ingredients:

- 2 Tbsp. oil
- 2 cups coconut milk
- 1 Tbsp. cinnamon powder or 2 inches bark broken/chopped into pieces
- 1 Tbsp. whole cumin
- 3 whole peppercorns
- 2 whole cloves
- 2 Tbsp. whole coriander seed powder
- Optional: 5 whole Kashmiri chilies (very special chilies that are not at all pungent; they give flavor and color but don't increase Pitta!)
- 1 cup mixed vegetables chopped in large pieces: carrots, snow peas, zucchini, broccoli
- 1 cup chopped starchy vegetable like sweet potato
- 1 Tbsp. turmeric powder
- 4 Tbsp. roughly ground almonds
- 3 Tbsp. Bragg's amino acid (replaces soy sauce with the fermentation or gluten)
- ½ Tbsp. lemon grass
- 1 Tbsp. brown sugar
- Optional: Shredded chili (not for Pitta)

Directions:

Grind and mix spices together or combine powders. Heat oil in a pot and sauté spices and vegetables in oil for a few minutes. Add only 1 cup of the coconut milk to the spice-vegetable mixture and cook until tender, then add a second cup of coconut milk, turmeric, and lemongrass.

Optional: Bragg amino acids (soy sauce alternative).

Moong Dhal Soup

- Dr. Sivanandani (Sivie) Pillay, PhD
Pietermaritzburg, KwaZulu Natal, South Africa

Dedicated to Dr. Pankaj Naram

I got to know about Dr. Naram through listening to a talk by Dr. Clint G. Rogers on TEDX. I was immediately drawn to Dr. Naram and began to research his work. I was drawn to him because of my late grandfather, Mr. G. Moodley, who hailed from India. As a young man, he came to South Africa as an indentured laborer. He had healing hands and helped a lot of people with their sprains, joint pains, ailments, etc. I never learned the art of Marmaa from him and deeply regret this.

After surgery to remove my left thyroid gland in 2019, I almost lost my voice. I was devastated as my job involved using my voice and communicating with children and adults. I managed to somehow contact Dr. Pankaj Naram and he made various dietary recommendations which I followed. My voice gradually improved. I began to follow him carefully and tried the moong dhal soup.

I love cooking and experimenting with variations of the moong dhal soup. Whenever I am tired or feel sick, I make the soup as it contains fiber, iron, potassium, calcium including vitamin, A, B, C, and E. I often make this soup for my grandson, Kaairav, who is 16 months old, and he loves it. The heart of my family is enjoying good food together. This has inspired me to post my moong dhal recipe, since my goal in life is to motivate and inspire others. My wish is that my moong dhal soup will help those on a healing journey.

Ingredients:

- 2 cups moong dhal beans (soaked and washed)
- 1 tsp. Himalayan salt
- 4 cups water
- 3 Tbsp. Ghee
- 1 cup onion, finely chopped
- ½ tsp. jeera (cumin) seeds
- ½ tsp. mustard seeds
- 1 clove crushed garlic
- 10 curry leaves
- 6 dried chilies (optional)
- Chopped coriander leaves
- ¼ tsp. turmeric powder

Directions:

- Place pot on stove, add 2 cups moong dhal beans, soaked & washed.
- Add: 1 tsp. pink Himalayan salt and 4 cups water. Bring to boil, add ¼ tsp. oil so it doesn't boil over.
- Add ½ tsp. turmeric powder and cook on high for 10 minutes.
- Reduce heat, cook on low for 30 - 40 minutes.
- If the water level is low, add hot water. When moong is soft, remove and drop into a dish and let cool. Wash the pot.
- Add 2 to 3 Tbsp. of Ghee to the clean pan. When Ghee is heated add jeera seeds and mustard seeds.
- Once popped add crushed garlic, chopped onion, curry leaves and ¼ tsp. turmeric powder, dried chilies (maybe 2 - I use about 6).
- Simmer on low for flavors to mix, stirring continuously. After about 15 minutes, add the moong dal beans. Let it boil on high for about 5 minutes. Reduce heat, simmer for 15 minutes.
- If the soup is thick, add more hot water to the preferred thickness.
- Add chopped coriander (cilantro) leaves as optional garnish

- You can add a different variety of vegetables when braising the ingredients (i.e., finely chopped carrots, green beans, and/or peas). You can add boiled lentils or channa (chickpeas) during braising.

Note: Some people with Pitta imbalance should avoid chilies. Check with your Ayushakti practitioner for your personal situation.

Sweet Potato, Carrot & Ginger Soup

- Carol Ray

Ingredients:

- 1 medium sweet potato (yam) peeled and cut in 1/2" cubes
- 1 medium onion peeled and diced
- 3 large organic carrots peeled and diced
- 3 stalks of organic celery cleaned and diced
- 1 slice of fresh ginger, peeled and pressed through garlic press
- 1 clove of garlic peeled and pressed
- 1 box (32 oz) of organic veggie broth or 4 cups of filtered water
- 1 small can (8 oz) of coconut milk (or almond or oat)
- Optional: Top with pepitas (pumpkin seeds), pecan pieces or walnut pieces for some crunch

Directions:

Start with a heaping tablespoon of Ghee in a soup pan on low heat. Add your choice of spices into the Ghee: cumin, coriander, turmeric, dash of cayenne, cinnamon, nutmeg, cloves, rosemary, bay leaf (remove before blending) or whatever you like using about ⅛ to ¼ tsp. (or more according to taste) each into the Ghee. Stir while they simmer for a few minutes to bring out the flavor.

Add the vegetables, stir well, then add water or broth; cook about an hour (adjust for high altitude and stove type) on low to medium-low until all veggies are soft, adding additional water if needed to keep soupy consistency; then blend in a blender or immersion blender until smooth. Slowly add room-temperature milk of choice to your desired thickness, blend in the blender on low, just until mixed well. Salt and pepper to taste. Add optional garnishes if desired.

Moong Dal Dosa

- Neha Singhania, Nepal

Ingredients:

- 2 cup Moong Dal
- ½ cup Urad (black lentil) Dal
- 1 cup cooked rice
- 10-15 fenugreek seeds
- 1 ½ tsp. salt
- A bit of Ghee or avocado oil
- Optional: Grated coconut or green coriander chutney

Directions:

Add 10-15 fenugreek seeds (methi) to the dal mixture (Moong Dal and Urad Dal) and let it soak for 5-6 hours. Make a thin paste of the soaked dal mixture and rice using a blender or food processor. Make a batter of the mixture by adding just a little water to make a medium thin batter like the ones used to make dosas. Add

1 ½ tsp. salt and let the batter set for an hour.

Use a Dosa or plain pan. Keep the pan heated on a medium flame. During the process, drizzle a little oil on the pan and a little water (7-8 drops). Spread the batter like making a pancake and put a little oil around the side of the pan. Wait for the batter to turn slightly golden in color and then spread a little oil on top of the batter. Let it settle for 2-3 minutes. Once the crispy Dosa is cooked, you can add any fillings (sweet potato, masala, vegetables, or paneer). Serve it with coconut or green coriander chutney.

Video: https://www.MyAncientSecrets.com/recipe/Taruns_Mom

Moong Bean Falafel

- Minerva Larios, Rialto, Ca, USA

After 2 months of eating the miracle moong bean I was ready for month 3 with the detox herbs and excited when my sister decided to join me. My sister, Barbara, was suffering from a list of health problems that included depression, anxiety, obesity, fatigue, and sleep apnea. After a case of Covid her doctor decided to send her for a sleep study. They learned that over the course of the night Barbara would stop breathing 123 times per hour and was given a breathing machine that she was to use for a minimum of 4 hours each night.

This sleep apnea was depriving her body of much needed rest and recovery. We were in disbelief when she stopped snoring by day 3. We couldn't believe that this was working so quickly, nor could we understand how 3 days of moong bean soup and some herbal remedies could fix this problem. It was an unexpected miracle! By day 20 she had also lost 15 lbs. You could see her body shrinking and each day the inflammation in her body and face was visibly reduced.

Note: I use a food processor because it gives me the texture and consistency that I want for a patty. The first attempt had Italian parsley and the 2nd didn't as I ran out. I preferred without, but it's part of the original falafel recipe.

Ingredients:

- 1 cup split moong or whole moong beans soaked overnight
- 1 bunch of cilantro - Note: I don't use stems
- 1 bunch of parsley, chopped, no stems
- 1 green Serrano chili (avoid if Pitta),
- ½ of a small red onion
- 1-2 garlic cloves (optional).
- ½ tsp. turmeric
- ½ tsp. of Asafoetida
- ½ tsp. of garam masala
- ½ to 1 tsp. of salt
- 1 tsp. of cumin
- 1 tsp. of coriander
- 1 tsp. of pomegranate powder (optional)

Directions:

- Drain and rinse your moong beans and add to a food processor along with the remaining ingredients

- Pulse until everything is fully combined and the mixture sticks together when lightly pressed.

- Cover and let sit for 10 mins.

- Preheat your oven to 175ºC / 350ºF and line a baking tray with baking (parchment) paper.

- Scoop about 2 tablespoons of mixture and use your hands to make it into a ball, placing it on the tray and lightly flattening the top. Repeat until there is no mixture left.

- Bake for 10 minutes, flip, and bake for a further 10 until the outside is golden and crisp. (Total 20 minutes) or pan fry 2 minutes per side in Ghee, avocado oil, or coconut oil.

Photo Credit: Keerty Das

Quinoa Buddha Bowl

- *Keerty Das*

Ingredients:

- Cooked quinoa: 1 cup
- Moong bean patties or falafel
- Spinach, Arugula for garnish
- Beetroot, grated
- Carrot, grated
- Assemble all the ingredients in a bowl and drizzle with tahini sauce and enjoy.

Note: raw vegetables are not recommended during a detox or when having any kind of "flare", but sometimes you can enjoy them grated or lightly sautéed to improve digestion.

Healthy Moong Dahl Pakoda / Falafel

- Dr. Smita Naram

Ingredients:

- ½ cup moong dal soaked overnight
- Masala mix: 1 tsp. whole coriander, 1 tsp. fennel, 1 tsp. whole cumin, ¼ tsp. whole black peppercorn, powdered on mortar and pestle or spice blender
- ¼ tsp. green chilies (optional, a little is good for digestion, too much is not good)
- 1 Tbsp. fresh coriander/cilantro
- ¼ tsp. sea salt

Directions:

Grind soaked and drained moong dal and let sit for a few hours (2+). Add masala spice mix, grated ginger, chilies (optional), cori-ander/cilantro leaves, and salt. Mix all together well. Heat a pan/Stuffed Pancake Pan/Aebleskiver for non-fried falafel, add a few drops of oil in pits, and pour mixture in each; sauté until golden brown and crispy on both sides and completely cooked inside. This can also be cooked in an air fryer. Enjoy with green chutney.

Side Dishes

Grilled Vegetables

- Carol Ray

Dr. Pankaj Naram would be the first to remind people that more vegetables in your diet will keep you healthier and help you to live longer. Many people don't seem to enjoy vegetables as often as they should because they do not know how to cook them. If you cook vegetables properly and add spices to your liking, you can enjoy eating cooked vegetables. Before reading *Ancient Secrets of a Master Healer,* my American diet consisted of lots of raw vegetables in salads. The result was a belly full of trouble! After consulting with the doctors at Ayushakti, I stopped eating raw vegetables (except occasional carrots and celery) and instead now eat vegetables roasted or mixed with moong (mung) beans and perhaps some rice. Not only am I fifteen pounds lighter but am also free of abdominal pain after eating and sticking to Dr. Pankaj Naram's diet: gluten, dairy, and sugar-free; very little meats; no sour fruits, no raw vegetables, and no nightshades.

Select organic, locally grown vegetables when possible. Good choices for grilling include asparagus, yellow crookneck squash, zucchini, sweet potato, carrots, onion, and bok choy. Wash and dry the fresh vegetables, peel the squash, sweet potato, and carrots; line a baking sheet with foil, arrange the sliced vegetables on the sheet.

Spray or drizzle with Ghee or oven-safe oil (avocado oil or coconut oil), just until slightly coated. Sprinkle salt, pepper, garlic, and other spices on the vegetables. Grill (broil) under close supervision on the lowest setting for 5-8 minutes. Turn and cook an additional 3-5 minutes. Serve warm.

Moong Bean (Mb) Hummus

- *Arati Malavalli-Majd,* Germany

As a vegetarian, I grew up with moong beans as a festive food and mostly, my parents cooked the traditional Indian meals. Otherwise, I must say that I loved moong beans always and now since following Dr. Clint G. Rogers for the past year I have been consuming moong dishes every day at least once every day and tried several new dishes.

I do enjoy all of them and my family also started enjoying a few of these recipes, mostly dosas. I recently participated in a 28-day cleanse with moong beans and the Healthiimi Detox™ by Ayushakti. I lost about 5kg (about 11 pounds) during the cleanse and felt my waistline slim down slightly. I was breathing better and had good stamina...Food means a lot to me, as I believe in "Let food be thy medicine," according to Hippocrates.

I do love to cook vegetarian and vegan dishes and love to have a variety daily. When I did the cleanse, within the first 3 days, I realized how my body was detoxing, meaning it was full of toxins from over the years.

Ingredients:

- 100 g (about a half-cup) of moong beans, whole green, or split with skin. Soak the split beans for 6 to 8 hours or the whole beans for 24 hours.
- 1 tsp. Ghee
- ½ tsp. mustard seeds & curcuma (turmeric) powder
- ⅛ tsp. asafetida (hing)
- 1 tsp. each of coriander seeds & cumin powder
- 1 Tbsp. tahini (sesame paste)
- 1 clove garlic
- 2 tsp. lime or lemon juice – omit depending on your Dosha
- 2 Tbsp. extra virgin olive oil
- 1 Tbsp. cilantro
- Green chilis to taste. Omit if you are Pitta Dosha
- Himalayan salt
- Crushed coriander seeds

Directions:

Melt Ghee in moderate heat, bring mustard seeds to crackle, add crushed coriander and hing as well as drained moong beans. Mix well with spices, add 300 ml (1.25 cups) water, cook for 3 to 5 minutes, salt thereafter, or at the end.

Add in the powdered spices, as well as tahini and lime, olive oil, cilantro, and mash when cooled.

Optional: If you want to skip cilantro use parsley or dill instead.

Moong Fruit Salad

- *Linda Tuma,* Oregon, USA

I was introduced to Dr. Clint G. Rogers and Master Healer Pankaj Naram's teachings by my daughter, Sara Morrell. Dr. Clint was to be a guest speaker at an event she was hosting. Although the event never happened due to Covid-19, it set off a chain of events I could never have predicted.

I had recently been diagnosed with severe osteoporosis at the age of 63. The treatments my doctor offered me (IV therapy) had tremendous side effects and I began seeking alternative treatments. I knew there had to be a better way, a healthier way to conquer this condition. Around this time, Dr. Clint's book came out, *"Ancient Secrets of a Master Healer: A Western Skeptic, An Eastern Master, And Life's Greatest Secrets."* The universe had sent me the answers I was seeking in this book.

Soon, my diet changed; not by giant leaps at first but by small steps. I don't let go easily. But over time the pendulum swayed. Suddenly I found myself ordering 40 pounds of organic moong beans, my cupboard was filled with jars of spices from faraway lands that I had never heard of before, and I was making Ghee. I was becoming a believer. I stopped buying meat and began always checking labels for wheat or sugar.... I hung signs on my refrigerator like this quote from Dr. Pankaj Naram: "If you change your food, you can change your future;" and I started taking an Ayushakti supplement, Painmukti Sandhi-cal™ for my osteoporosis. My husband always had a dislike for anything organic or healthy. His diet was potato chips, Pepsi, and candy bars. They took a toll on his body, and he had been recently diagnosed with congestive heart failure. I started listening to Dr. Clint's Ancient Secrets Foundation "SUNDAY INSPIRATION CALLS" and a miracle happened: my husband had been listening in and suddenly decided to give up his old way of eating and embrace this new healthier lifestyle!

We stripped the house of anything containing red meat, wheat, or sugar, replacing our previous diet with moong beans and vegetables. He even started walking every day. To date he has dropped over 20 lbs. and is working on improving his health following Master Healer Pankaj Naram's guidelines.

Today I am inspired every time I open my computer and I see the quote from page 77 of Ancient Secrets of a Master Healer: "The Great Secret for Succeeding at Anything —That may be true, but most people do not actually give 100 percent, because they are lazy or afraid of failing. When you start to actually give 100 % in everything you do, a different quality of enjoyment comes into your life, fear lessens, and you start to see very different results."

With emotional healing I find the more I value my self-worth, the more willing I am to put the effort into changing. It is the quote I hear every Sunday that inspires me to love myself and open my perspective to the healing art of Vedic-based healing practices: - "I didn't come to teach you. I came to love you. Love will teach you."

- Linda Tuma

Ingredients:

Sauce

- ½ cup yellow moong beans
- 1 can coconut cream
- 1 tsp. vanilla
- ½ tsp. cinnamon
- ½ tsp. allspice
- ¼ tsp. nutmeg
- 1 Tbsp. honey
- 1 tsp. celery seeds
- 1 tsp. sesame seeds
- ¼ tsp. salt

Salad:

- 1 cup cold cooked sticky rice - I used paella rice (slightly salted)

- 3 bananas
- 1 large cucumber (deseeded), approx.2 cups
- 1 avocado
- ¾ cup apple
- ¾ cup Garbanzo beans* (best for Kapha & Pitta)
- 10 leaves of fresh mint
- Sliced almonds to garnish

Directions:

Cook yellow moong beans until softened. Drain if necessary. Let cool.

Mix cooled moong beans with all the sauce ingredients in a food processor, process until creamy, adding enough coconut cream to achieve desired thickness.

Then cube the cucumber, bananas, avocado, and apple.

Mix all the ingredients together and top with Moong sauce. Garnish with mint and sliced almonds (which are good for people with Pitta).

*Garbanzo beans are high in air and space energy, and most Vata-types should avoid them. For Kapha and Pitta types, they can help to reduce body inflammation and swelling. Use raw cucumbers with caution, depending on your digestion.

Pesto Sauce

- Rosa Ramirez

Ingredients:

- ½ cup walnuts
- 3 cloves of garlic, minced
- 3 cups packed fresh basil leaves
- 1 cup spinach leaves
- Juice of ½ lemon (omit if aggravated Pitta or Kapha)
- 1 to 1 ½ cups extra-virgin olive oil
- ¼ to ½ teaspoon salt
- ½ teaspoon black pepper

Directions:

Heat a dry skillet over medium-high heat; when the pan is hot, add the walnuts in a single layer and stir or shake frequently until lightly browned, about 2 minutes. Combine the walnuts and garlic in a food processor and pulse a few times to combine. Add the basil and spinach and pulse until coarsely chopped. Add the lemon juice.

While mixing on low speed, add the olive oil, in a slow stream until all the ingredients are fully blended. Add the salt, pepper, and pulse a few more times to combine. Store in the refrigerator for up to 2 to 3 days in ice cube trays.

HINT: Traditional pesto uses pine nuts, but these can be expensive. You can substitute whatever type of nuts you have on hand, like pecans or almonds.

Curry Leaf & Cilantro Chutney

- Dr. Smita Naram

Ingredients:

- 8 to 10 fresh curry leaves
- ¼ cup raw almonds (best if soaked and peeled)
- 1½ to 2-inch piece of ginger, peeled (grated if needed)
- ½ to 1 cup water, according to preference
- 2 cups tightly packed fresh cilantro
- ¼ teaspoon Himalayan salt
- Juice of ½ lime (omit if aggravated Pitta or Kapha)

Directions:

Blend all ingredients together to a paste.

Source: Dr. Smita Naram and Lisa Cagan Mitchell

https://sacredanddelicious.com/2016/04/08/easy-curry-leaf-chutney/

Vegan Pesto

- Dr. Pankaj Naram

Ingredients:

- 2 cups, washed, loosely packed stemmed fresh herbs - basil, cilantro, parsley, mint
- ½ cup shelled pecans or walnuts or pine nuts
- 1-2 cloves fresh garlic
- ¼ to ½ cup good tasting extra virgin olive oil, as needed
- Sea salt, to taste

Directions:

- Step 1: Combine the fresh herbs, nuts, and garlic in a food processor and process the mixture until it turns into a coarse meal.
- Step 2: Slowly add extra virgin olive oil in a steady drizzle as you pulse the processor on and off. Process until it becomes a smooth, light paste. Add enough olive oil to keep it moist and spreadable.
- Season with sea salt, to taste.
- Cover and store chilled for at least an hour to saturate the flavors. I like to pour a this layer of extra virgin olive oil over the top to help keep it bright green.
- Makes roughly a rounded cup.

Note: pesto can darken if heated (basil turns black when hot) so add it to hot dishes (like cooked pasta) at the very last minute if the color is important to you.

About Lime:

Pacifies Vata, Pitta, and Kapha. Clear, cold, light, liquefied. Moves energy downward, then outward. General laxative and stool softener. Detoxicant. Improves focus.

Beverages

About Beverages

You can drink tea and coffee, but herbal or green tea and decaffeinated coffee are better. Good alternatives to real coffee are Caro, Barley Cup, or dandelion (dandelion is a diuretic) coffee. Ginger tea made from fresh roots is warming, Agni increasing, removes mucus and toxins and is the best remedy for coughs and colds. Plain hot water is also good for clearing the digestive tract, especially first thing in the morning.

Fresh vegetable and fruit juices are very nourishing but should be avoided in cold weather or while suffering from colds. Giving up iced beverages with meals is a definite challenge for many people, especially Southerners in the US and their iced tea! But expect great improvements in your digestion when you stop putting out the digestive fire with ice cold drinks.

Teas

Dr. Naram's Ginger Tea

Ginger water is the ideal remedy when you have a cough, cold or excess mucus accumulation in your throat and sinuses. Being hot in nature, ginger can cut into and loosen mucus as well as stimulate the digestive fire so that the stomach can clear the mucus effectively. Due to this stimulating action on digestion, it is also the perfect drink to be taken either before a meal or half an hour afterwards.

Cut 4-5 slices of fresh ginger root and place in a pan of water. Bring it to a boil and allow it to simmer for at least 5 minutes. Strain into a mug and enjoy! If you wish to sweeten it with honey, add it only after the liquid has cooled to a slightly warm temperature as honey is not heat stable.

Yogi Tea – Ralph Brown

This is the original recipe given by Yogi Bhajan. For 2 cups, start with 20 oz. of water. For convenience, make at least 4 cups at one time, so you may wish to double the following:

To two cups of boiling water, add:

- ½ tsp. whole cloves
- 4 whole green cardamom pods
- ¼ tsp. whole black peppercorns
- 1 stick cinnamon (4")
- 4 thin slices of fresh ginger
- ½ tsp. black or green tea
- 1 cup milk (oat, coconut, almond, or rice)
- Local honey or coconut sugar (to taste)

Directions:

Gently boil for 15-minutes, then add 1/2 tsp. of any black or green tea. Let sit for one or two minutes and then add ½ cup milk (almond milk, oat, rice, or coconut) and reheat. Strain and serve with honey or coconut sugar to taste.

Black pepper is a blood purifier, cardamom is for the colon (gas), cloves are for the nervous system and cinnamon for the bones. Ginger has a delicious taste and is helpful when suffering from a cold, recovering from the flu or for general physical weakness.

Milk aids in the easy assimilation of the spices and avoids irritation to the colon. The black or green tea acts as an alloy for all the ingredients, achieving a new chemical structure which makes the tea a healthful and delicious drink.

Basil Herb Tea

- 10 fresh basil leaves
- A few long pieces of fresh ginger
- ¼ tsp. black pepper powder
- ¼ tsp. turmeric powder
- 2-inch-long piece of cinnamon (or ¼ tsp. cinnamon powder)
- 2 cardamom pods
- Boil in a cup of water for 5 min. Drink lukewarm.

Three Options for Detox Tea

1. Summer Tea (cooling):

- 2 cups of water
- ⅔ tsp. cumin seed
- ⅔ tsp. coriander seed
- ⅔ tsp. fennel seed

Combine herbs with two cups of water (CCF Tea: Cumin, Coriander, Fennel). Bring to a boil, then reduce heat, strain, and enjoy.

You can make a large batch for the day, or smaller servings, every 2-3 hours throughout the day. This detox tea can be enjoyed throughout the detox. You can adjust the strength of the tea to suit your taste.

2. Winter Tea (warming):

2 tsp. of dry ginger powder added to five (5) glasses (about a liter) of water. Bring it to a boil, let it cool down, and drink it warm, hourly, throughout the day.

TIP: If you are out of ground ginger you will need to know how fresh to use. In general, one (1) tablespoon of chopped fresh herbs is equivalent to ¼ teaspoon of the dried, powdered version.

3. All Season Tea

- 2 tsp. dry ginger powder
- 2 tsp. cumin powder
- 2 tsp. coriander powder
- 2 tsp. fennel powder

Bring 8 cups of water to a boil. Add the herbs, let steep, then transfer to a thermos to keep warm throughout the day.

Smoothies

Option 1: Mint/Coriander

1 glass of mint coriander (cilantro) juice - take 1 handful fresh mint leaves + 1 handful fresh coriander leaves, add to a 10-ounce glass of water, and blend until smooth, then add salt and pepper to taste.

Option 2: Apple/Carrot/Beetroot

- Take 1 medium-sized apple
- ½ beetroot (optional)
- 1 cup carrot cubes
- 1-inch piece peeled ginger

- Add 1 glass of water and then blend all the ingredients in the blender until the desired consistency. You may prefer to strain it.

Option 3: Tridosha Smoothie

- 1 Cabbage (if Pitta/Kapha) or spinach (if Vata)
- 2 Carrots
- 1 Apple/pomegranate
- Make one glass of juice
- Add half tsp. of organic turmeric powder
- Drink 3-6 glasses of juice every day

Almond Milk: Homemade Raw

- Dr. Pankaj Naram

Ingredients:

- 1 cup raw almonds
- Water for soaking nuts
- 3 cups water
- 2 dates (optional)
- ½ tsp. vanilla (optional)

Directions:

- Soak the almonds in water overnight or for at least 6 hours. Remove the skins from the soaked almonds.
- Drain the water from the almonds and discard.
- Blend the 3 cups of water, almonds, and dates until well blended and almost smooth.
- Strain the blended almond mixture using cheesecloth or other strainer.
- Homemade raw almond milk will keep well in the refrigerator for three or four days. Enjoy!

Homemade Electrolytes

- Carol Ray

An alternative to expensive store-bought options

- 3 cups cold organic coconut water
- Pea-size portion of peeled grated ginger
- ⅛ cup pure organic maple syrup (omit if diabetic)
- 2 tablespoons cranberry, pomegranate, or cherry juice
- ⅛ teaspoon mineral salt (use less if you only have table salt)

Coconut water contains calcium and potassium (about 16x more potassium than Gatorade!). Drink up to 20 ounces per day. Any more than that can cause diarrhea in some people.

Pure maple syrup contains calcium, potassium, iron, zinc, and manganese. Mineral salt, while being mostly sodium, contains 60+ trace minerals! Sodium is an important electrolyte to replenish. It is critical for maintaining fluid balance, nerve function, and for muscle contractions.

Sweets

Puffed Rice Ladoo

- *Esther Wolkowitz,* Los Angeles, CA

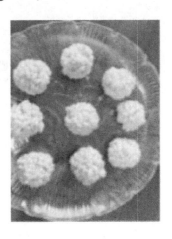

I spent 17 days at Ayushakti doing Panchakarma. The experience was life changing and I have never felt so nourished and cared for in my life. It was moong soup for breakfast and dinner and a tali plate (assorted veggies) for lunch. My extra treats were papaya at breakfast and after 2 weeks I had fresh pomegranate juice in the afternoon.

While there I was able to take cooking lessons with the chef at the on-site café. I learned many dishes that I was not eating but that I have now enjoyed making for myself and friends at home. The Ladoo is a sweet treat - almost like Rice Krispy Treats but healthier!

Ingredients:

- 1 cup jaggery (light color is best)
- ½ tsp. cardamom powder
- 4 tsp. sesame seed
- 4 cups puffed rice

Directions:

Heat the empty pot until hot. Turn down the burner and then slowly melt the jaggery in a hot pot. Do NOT use any water. When melted, add the rest of the ingredients into the melted jaggery. Stir until coated.

Form coated puffed rice into 2-inch balls while the mixture is still very warm. YUM!

Note: Use powdered jaggery, not whole. You might like to add more cardamom powder.

Moong Bean Brownies

- Esther Wolkowitz

Ingredients:

- 1 ½ cups of cooked moong beans
- ½ cup cacao powder
- ½ cup quick oats
- 10 pitted Medjool dates
- ½ cup hot water for dates
- ¼ cup maple syrup
- ¼ cup plant-based milk
- 1 tsp. vanilla extract
- 1 tsp. baking powder
- ⅛ tsp. baking soda
- ¼ tsp. salt
- ½ to 1 cup dark chocolate chips

Directions:

1. Preheat oven to 350F. Line 8"x 8" baking pan with parchment paper

2. Soak the dates in ½ cup of hot water for at least 20 minutes. Then add ¼ cup maple

syrup, ¼ cup plant-based milk, moong, and vanilla to the dates and water. Add cacao powder, oats, and salt.

3. In food processor or blender combine all ingredients except chocolate chips and blend until smooth

4. Stir in chocolate chips and spread the batter evenly in the prepared pan. (Batter may be a bit crumbly and that is okay).

5. Sprinkle some extra chocolate chips on top

6. Bake 16-20 minutes until the center of the toothpick comes out clean. Allow it to cool before slicing. Store in an airtight container.

Ancient Secrets Chocolate Frosting

- Punam Patel, Los Angeles

Ingredients:

- ¼ cup of almond butter
- 2 Tbsp. cacao powder
- ¼ cup raw maple syrup
- 2-3 small pieces of dark chocolate
- ¼ cup plant-based milk

Directions:

Combine the wet ingredients with the dry ingredients and mix well. Add to a small pan and bring to low heat, stirring constantly until the mixture reaches a smooth, velvet-like consistency. Use after the brownies (or whatever needs some chocolate frosting) have cooled down, at about 10 minutes.

Double Chocolate Black Bean Brownies

- Ellen Saraswati

Ingredients:

- 3 cups black beans (2 15-oz organic can, drained & rinsed very well)
- 4 Tbsp. cocoa powder
- 1 cup quick oats
- ½ tsp. sea salt
- 2/3 cup pure maple syrup or organic pure agave
- ½ cup pure organic coconut oil or organic cow's Ghee
- 4 tsp. pure alcohol-free vanilla extract
- 1 tsp. baking powder
- 1 cup to 1 ¼ cup dark chocolate chips (for less sweet taste I use semi-sweet dark chocolate)

Optional: more chips, for decoration. Yield: 9-12 brownies

Directions:

- Preheat oven to 350 F.
- Combine all ingredients (except chocolate chips) in a good food processor or a powerful blender, and blend until completely smooth.
- Stir in the chocolate chips, then pour into a greased 8×8 pan.
- Sprinkle or arrange the extra chocolate chips over the top.
- Bake the black bean brownies for 25 minutes, then let cool at least 10 minutes before trying to cut. If they still look a bit undercooked, you can place them in the fridge overnight and they will magically firm up!

Banana Coconut Oatmeal Cookies

- *Suzanne Maitszen,* Utah, USA

I was looking for a recipe that is healthy for my 15- and 18-year-old boys, both are mostly plant based. I saw a peanut butter oatmeal recipe that had sugar and other items I did not agree with. Peanut

Butter has too much fat, so I came up with this recipe.

Gluten free, fat free, sugar free loaded with healthy ingredients like cinnamon, bananas, protein powder & lots of Love for my growing and always hungry boys.

If you want the cookies to be sweeter and not concerned about sugar, you can add regular chocolate chips, and if not concerned with fat add 2 tablespoons of crunchy peanut butter.

Ingredients:

- 2 ripe bananas
- 2 scoops any vegan vanilla protein powder (optional)
- 2 cups quick cooking oats

- ½ cup plant-based milk (I like chocolate oat or almond milk)
- 4 Tbsp. unsweetened shredded coconut
- 3 Tbsp. chocolate chips
- 2 tsp. cinnamon
- 2 tsp. vanilla extract
- ¼ cup nuts of your choice (I use walnuts, sunflower, or pumpkin seeds)
- 1 Tbsp. cocoa powder (optional) & lots and lots and lots of LOVE

Directions:

Preheat the oven to 325 F. Mix everything together. Scoop cookies onto cookie sheet, place in oven, bake for about 20 minutes.

8 Ingredient Cardamom & Rose Cookies

- *Kalie Malky*

Total Time: 12 mins   Servings: 16

Ingredients:

- 3 cups (360 g) almond meal or ground whole almonds
- 4 tablespoons extra virgin olive oil
- 5 ½ tablespoons organic maple syrup
- 2 tablespoons rosewater
- 1 teaspoon ground cardamom
- 1 teaspoon vanilla extract or powder
- ½ teaspoon baking powder
- ½ teaspoon sea salt flakes
- Crushed pistachios and dried rose petals for topping

Directions:

- Ofen auf 190°C (Ober-/Unterhitze) / 170°C (Umluft) vorheizen.
- Line a rimmed baking sheet with baking paper.

- Place almond meal, olive oil, maple syrup, rosewater, cardamom, vanilla, baking powder and salt in a medium bowl. Using your hands, knead the mixture into a dough.

- Take about a tablespoon of mixture and roll it into a ball. Place on the prepared sheet and flatten with the palm of your hand. Repeat for the remaining mixture. You should get about 16 cookies.

- Press crushed pistachios and rose petals on top of each cookie. When you do this, the edges might flare and crack, just pinch together and smooth the edges.

- Bake in pre-heated oven for 10-12 minutes (for chewy cookies) or 14 minutes (for crispier cookies).

Notes:

The cookie dough can be eaten raw. It will keep in the fridge for up to two weeks and in the freezer for up to 2 months. The recipe can be easily halved (every single ingredient halved exactly). That will result in 8 cookies. When halving the recipe, bake only for 8-10 minutes at 190°C.

Note: Use mild flavored olive oil for this recipe.

Baked Pears with Goat's Cheese

- *Carol Ray*

Pears are rich in folate, vitamin C and K, copper and potassium as well as being a good source of polyphenol antioxidants. This is a beautiful desert to serve guests.

Ingredients:

- 1 organic red pear serves two people
- ½ cup filtered water
- 2 ounces of goat's cheese (divided)
- 2 tablespoons blue agave or similar syrup (maple, molasses, etc.)
- 1 tablespoon chopped pecans or walnuts (divided)
- Sprinkle of ground cinnamon (optional)

Directions:

Preheat the oven to 425 degrees F. Carefully cut the pear in half lengthwise, leaving stem and seeds. Line a baking dish with foil for easy clean up, then place the pears cut side down on the foil. Add water and bake for about 20 minutes, depending on the size of your pears; pears should be very soft, but still intact.

Remove from the oven and turn the pears over on the foil. Carefully remove the stem and seeds from the center and scoop out a bit of the pulp to create a small cavity. In a small bowl, mix goat's cheese with syrup and nuts. Place mixture on top of pear halves and sprinkle lightly with cinnamon if desired.

Gluten-Free Breads

Sunflower/Sesame Crackers

- Carol Ray

Ingredients:

- 1 cup sunflower seeds
- 1 cup sesame seeds
- small amount of filtered water, just enough to make a paste Optional: dried herbs such as parsley, thyme, basil, sea salt, black pepper, garlic powder, cinnamon, etc.

Directions:

Preheat oven to 200 degrees F. Place sunflower seeds in a food processor and pulse to a flour consistency. Be careful not to pulse for too long as it will become sunflower seed butter. Transfer to a bowl and add the sesame seeds to the mix. Stir to combine evenly. Add water in small amounts (8-10 tablespoons, more if it seems dry) and stir the mixture well, stopping when the flour and water have come together into a mass of dough.

Line a baking sheet with parchment paper and place the dough on top. Top with another sheet of parchment paper, and, with a rolling pin, roll out the dough as thinly as possible, ensuring thickness is consistent. Remove the upper sheet of parchment paper and sprinkle the dough with salt, pepper, herbs, as desired. Score the dough into desired shapes with a sharp knife. Do not cut all the way through the dough, just deep enough to help break the crackers apart once baked.

Bake until golden and the center is crisp, about 20 - 30 minutes. Turn the oven off, open the door slightly, and leave to cool to help dry out the crackers for maximum crunch. Once completely cooled, break along the score lines, serve, or store in an airtight container.

Adapted from Girl Gone Primal: Recipe: Sunflower Sesame Crackers

Gluten-Free Roti / Flatbread

- *Aparna Yardi,* Cincinnati, Ohio

Ingredients:

- 1 cup jowar/sorghum flour
- ¾ cup water
- salt to taste
- ½ cup jowar flour for dusting

Directions:

1. Bring the water to boil. When the water begins to boil, add some salt. Turn off the flame and add the flour to this boiling water. Mix with a spoon while the water is very hot.

2. Cover this mixture and let it rest and cool for about 30 minutes.

3. When it is still a little warm knead with your hand; you may have to sprinkle a little water.

4. Make equal size balls out of the dough.

5. Dust the rolling surface with some flour.

6. Dip the dough in flour and flatten it by patting it slowly with your hand; you may need to add some flour. I cut open a zip- lock bag and place

the dough in the bag and then use a rolling pin over the zip-lock bag to roll the dough.

7. Put the griddle on the flame and once hot, put the flattened dough onto the griddle

8. Now dip a cloth or brush in water and start wiping the top surface of the flatbread.

9. Wait until water evaporates and then flip it on to the other side.

10. Press gently with a ladle to fluff; now remove it from the griddle.

11. Note: each side should be roasted light brown in color.

12. I sometimes use finger millet (Ragi) flour, Amaranth flour, and make flatbread using the same process.

Easy & Healthy Bread

- Carol Ray

Ingredients:

- 4 eggs
- 1 tsp. baking soda
- 1 cup tahini
- Pinch of salt
- Optional: cranberries or blueberries

Directions:

Beat the eggs well in a deep bowl. Stir in the baking soda, tahini, and salt. Mix well. Pour the mixture into mini loaf pan or 8" cake pan (lined with parchment paper or spray with olive, safflower, or avocado oil). Place pan in a preheated oven at 350 degrees F for25-30 minutes. Before baking, you can als o try mixing in fruits like blueberries or cranberries, a few seasonal spices, perhaps agave or maple syrup, with a bit of grated orange rind, for holidays. I cooked the cranberries like a chutney, in a half cup of water, with maple syrup, and a pinch of cinnamon before adding into the bread dough. After baking, you can add Ghee with herbs like garlic, ground pepper, and ground rosemary for example, and serve with a plate of extra virgin olive oil with ground pepper mixed in it.

Bonus Materials

Ghee and Clarified Butter

While some people use the terms interchangeably, there are differences including:

- Taste: Ghee, which requires several hours more cooking time and the removal of the solids, has a nutty flavor.

- Regional preferences: Ghee originated in India and is popular in several other Asian cuisines, while clarified butter is more likely to be found in France. Called beurre noisette, or brown butter, created by not straining out the solids in the cooking process and cooking it less.

How to Make Ghee

Many of the ancient healing stories about Master Jivaka involved the use of Ghee as a remedy. If you only make one change to better your health, for most Dosha types, adding a teaspoon of Ghee to your morning routine can make a big difference in your digestion, skin tone, blood vessels, and so much more. Be sure and use medicinal Ghee, and not clarified butter.

To make Ghee, using the method proposed by Dr. Maranjii, use 4 pounds* of unsalted and organic, good quality butter. Place the butter in a heavy 6-quart enameled cast iron pot (not aluminum) and let it melt and simmer on the lowest possible heat.

If your simmer setting is too high, possible solutions are to use a sturdy cake pan ring that the pot sits on or using a comal (tortilla warmer) to disburse the heat if it can be done safely. Use a splatter guard if you have one.

At first, it will sputter and make a lot of noise; excessive sputtering means the heat is too high; the butter will look thick and cloudy, and foam will appear on the top. Do not stir or disturb the foam as it creates a barrier that is important to regulate the temperature.

Three hours on simmer should produce small bubbles; do not stir, remove foam, or disturb. Do not put a lid on it!

The Amazing Healing Powers of Medicinal Ghee

Continue cooking for 9 to 12 hours, depending on your stove and temperature settings.

At this point, the cooking process is complete. Use a very fine sieve, a double layer of cheesecloth or muslin over a crockery pot or alternatively a clean canning jar with an airtight lid that will contain the Ghee.

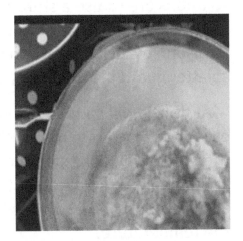

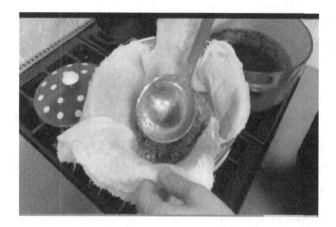

Cautiously use a large ladle to gently move the contents of the pot into the cheesecloth, being careful not to allow any of the sediment on the bottom of the pan to enter the jar. (The sediment will cause the Ghee to turn rancid.)

Do not place the top on the jar until totally cooled down.

Alternative Slow Cooker Method for Making Ghee

Alternatively, put it in a slow cooker for up to 9 hours (or overnight). Slowly heat the butter; fat particles will sink to the bottom, the foam will diminish on top, and the pure butter oil will become clear. The moment the sputtering stops, and the sediment on the bottom of the pan starts to turn golden or light brown, remove the pan from the heat, and let it cool down.

Notes: Quantity and quality of the unsalted butter, as well as the stove and pot used to cook It, can drastically affect the outcome of the recipe. Adjust times accordingly. Do not use aluminum pots and pans. Do not cover the pan. Ghee can be safely stored in the pantry in an air-tight jar. Best practice: take a small amount out for use during the week.

Do NOT mix Ghee and honey in equal measures.

Video: https://youtu.be/5VRrtOgBai8

Making Moong Soup Delicious

(Submitted from people around the world)

Once you create a fantastic soup with the basic recipe, you may want to experiment with slight alterations and variations. You can try these suggestions to create your ideal soup and/or discover options on how to switch things up to create multiple versions of Moong soup for a bit of fun! These tips and tricks from people around the world with their adaptations help make mouth-watering moong bean soup.

Andrea K.:
Adding Ghee-roasted onions sprinkled on top of the soup gives it an extra tasty kick.

Onions change their characteristics once they are softly roasted in Ghee and become sweet. The sweet taste gives power to the body and lowers the Vata Dosha. And/or try adding cardamom and fennel powder when roasting the masala ingredients in Ghee at the beginning.

Mike S:
I pop the mustard seeds in the Instant Pot in Ghee then add ginger and garlic until browned slightly. Then I add the rest of the spices and am prepared to add water as soon as needed to prevent burning.

Then add already cooked moong beans and other veggies as desired with more water: carrots, celery, beetroots, and string beans!!! It's amazing - the added veggie ingredients are from Ayushakti Dr. Priyanka: French beans, beetroot, carrots, and celery (but she said no potatoes or sweet potatoes are allowed for me).

Clare and Mark D.:
Our secret is to add fresh collard greens, kale, and chard from the garden, garam masala, and extra black mustard seeds.

Geeta:
Kokum & tamarind just add sourness to the dish (Note: Tamarind and other sour and fermented foods are discouraged. Kokum is great for giving the same kind of flavor and helps with digestion.)

Indraini M:
If you like you could add a pinch or two of hing or asafetida, the spice that helps in digestion and prevents gas. It has a strong aroma so add cautiously.

Jon D:
For me, the easiest and tastiest thing I have done is add some Lawry's Casero Adobo Seasoning! I like the one with pepper, but it seems they have a

version without it. (Note: Always read ingredients on extra spices and look for additives - keep it pure for detoxing.)

Mandy P:

Doubling up on ginger and garlic have helped me. Also, I notice that some kinds of Ghee I like much better than other kinds.

Linda:

Add to original moong bean soup recipe:

- 1 can coconut milk, 1 head cauliflower, and
- 2 Tbsp. Shawarma Seasoning.

Marie S:

We add all kinds of vegetables to our soup, varying every time so it doesn't get boring - carrots, broccoli, zucchini, yams, celery, and spinach.

Paige H:

Best thing I have done for taste is double or triple onion, garlic & veggies.

Shyama D:

I sprout the beans, cook, and cool them; put them in a blender until creamy. They are placed back in the pot, then spices are added and cooked some more for it to be blended and creamy.

Arati M:

I do use soaked and sprouted moong beans and keep them ready for topping any soup, salad, or omelet, mixing into idlis and vadas. Any mixed vegetables can be added. (Note: There is some debate regarding if sprouting is better or not. In general, Dr. Pankaj Naram did not encourage people to sprout the beans first. Sometimes sprouting the beans first makes it so there is more gas. If sprouting, cooking them will take away this problem.)

Tips for Reducing Gas and Bloating

(Submitted from people around the world)

Julia G:

While soaking moong beans overnight is the basic recommendation, soaking longer and rinsing them a few times, adding new water, helps eliminate gas. I like to soak the beans for about 32 hours to get the texture I like, having used 1 tsp. raw sugar in the first soak, and replacing water twice. I have had no problem since I started this. I have also used 1 tsp. baking soda doing the same process.

Aparna Y:

It was recommended by my Ayushakti doctor to use Moong Dahl (split and de-husked whole green moong beans) to prevent gas.

Jane W:

I have found that rinsing the beans very well before soaking them and then soaking for 6-8 or 12 hours works well. Ideally, I change the water every 2-3 hours and rinse them very well before cooking them which helps a lot. It took some time for me to learn how to stop being gassy.

Jon D:

Add 1 Tbsp. raw cane sugar to soaking moong beans at least 24 hours until the hulls crack, then add hing and kokum. Most will not experience gas. We all have different GI systems, but the suggestions so far have been like magic for most.

Also, here is an ancient healing tea recommended to me which can help reduce gas...

- 1 tsp. Jeera powder (cumin)
- ½ tsp. Shunthi (ginger)
- ¼ tsp. Ajwain (carom or Bishop's weed)
- ½ tsp. black salt
- 1 pinch Hing (Asafoetida)

Mix all in half a glass of water and have two times a day after food. If you have a lot of gas, have it 4 times a day. Add 1 tsp. raw sugar or baking soda to moong beans while soaking overnight. Dump out the water and rinse before cooking. Also, some people have reported that if they sprout the beans, it creates more gas, so I prefer using un- sprouted whole green moong. If you forgot to soak the beans overnight, it can help to parboil them 3 times before cooking (you put the beans in water on the stove until the water just barely boils, then strain out the water, add new water, and do it again 3 times.)

Ken W:

Add a few dates. Let the beans soak for half a day until they become alive. Put in baking soda while soaking to reduce lectins.

Linda:

For reducing sulfur causing gas issues, soak and cook the beans with 1 Tbsp. anise seeds or kombu seaweed.

Mindi S:

Soak the beans in raw sugar and apple cider vinegar.

Alison S:

If you are experiencing gas the following guidelines may help:

- Soak beans for longer (up to 18 hours) and rinse them several times, add 1 tsp. baking soda and kelp when soaking beans. Don't use sprouted beans if sensitive to gas.

- Additional remedies can be offered to help with gas. Gas will get better over time.

- You can cook multiple batches and freeze daily portions but don't keep soup for more than 1 night in the refrigerator and when you do overnight it in the refrigerator, add fresh spices.

- InstantPot™ or pressure cooker strongly reduces the time to cook.

- Pancakes with moong flour is also an option.

- Also I love the idea of thinking of Dr. Pankaj Naram as I cook and eat moong beans, adding love in the process.

- Moong beans come in yellow and green forms—find the one you like best.

Camille T

I just graduated from a plant-based natural chef school for which I've since been recruited to teach and wanted to share what we learned about bean cookery there in case it could be helpful to anyone still struggling.

Moong beans are among the quickest to cook and most easily digestible of beans (compared to the bigger beans, like kidney beans or chickpeas). Some of my teachers would say even soaking could potentially be left out for these beans, particularly if cooking them in a pressure cooker. However, to maximize digestibility, the following steps can be very helpful:

- SOAKING: Wash and then soak beans for 6-8 hours. Toss out the soak water and rinse the beans to remove any residue of what difficult- to-digest constituents were extracted by the soak water.

- PARBOILING AFTER SOAKING: Cover the beans with additional water (.5-1 inch above the bean line in a pressure cooker; 2 inches above the beans if you'll be steeping/boiling them in a regular pot) and bring them to an active boil with the lid off, for 5-10 minutes.

Scoop off any foam/scum that the beans give off during this process. (My teachers say these are part of the difficult-to-digest secondary compounds present in beans and you can imagine that same foamy/gassy reaction is taking place in your intestines if you leave them in there.) No need to toss the water - as long as you scoop off the foam, you can cook the beans in the water that remains after parboiling has caused an expected amount of it to evaporate (the water line should be no lower than the bean line if pressure cooking, a bit higher than the bean line if steeping in a regular pot).

- COOK THE BEANS WITH A DIGESTIVE AID: Different cultures use different plants to help break down/neutralize the difficult-to-digest secondary compounds in beans and aid in their digestion. We were trained to use .5 - 1in of kombu per cup of dry beans (in a more macrobiotically/Japanese-inspired program). It seems Hing/Asafoetida would be the Indian/ ayurvedic equivalent. If using kombu, rinse off any salty residue and add it to the beans before you cover them for cooking – it should cook with the beans. (Not sure how hing works yet but it seems adding it in for cooking towards the end with the rest of the spices is what's recommended in the book.)

NO SALT UNTIL AFTER THE BEANS ARE COOKED THROUGH

As far as the teachings I received go, while salt is instrumental in breaking down the cellular components of vegetables and grains during the first stages of their cooking, beans are an exception to this rule and adding salt in the first stage is purported to reinforce their self-defense mechanisms, rendering them more difficult to cook, and by extension to digest.

Cook them (pressure cooking or steeping) in water with a digestive aid (kombu-Japan, hing-India, epazote-Mexico, etc.) and AFTER they are cooked through, integrate the salt - at the same time as you add the Ghee-toasted spices & the vegetables, in this recipe - and let cook together for at least 10 minutes. [I know this is a controversial point in the cooking world, but if people are struggling, it's another thing they can experiment with and see what works for them.

About Dairy and Eggs

• The first and probably most important dietary advice that we learn from Dr. Pankaj Naram is to avoid milk and dairy products, except Ghee. Due to the process of preparing Ghee, the milk solids are removed, and Ghee transforms into a medicinal formula with amazing healing properties to balance all three Doshas: Vata, Pitta, and Kapha.

• Dr. Naram recommends 1 teaspoon of Ghee daily, added to a cup of warm water, even in the case of people with high cholesterol. Studies confirm the claim that Ghee taken in small amounts benefits the body[1].

• Fresh soft cheese such as cottage cheese, ricotta cheese, goat's cheese, fresh feta cheese, and Paneer are preferred for occasional consumption.

• Eggs are not considered dairy; they are a good source of protein. Eggs are good for Vata types as they are heating, heavy, unctuous (oily), and energizing. It is important not to eat eggs with dairy as it complicates digestion. Pitta and Kapha would benefit from sticking to egg whites, as yolks are heating.

[1] Sharma H, Zhang X, Dwivedi C. The effect of ghee (clarified butter) on serum lipid levels and microsomal lipid peroxidation. Ayu. 2010 Apr;31(2):134-40. doi: 10.4103/0974-8520.72361. PMID: 22131700; PMCID: PMC3215354.

About Grains

The following grains can be taken:

- Millet
- Amaranth
- Quinoa
- Kamut
- Sorghum
- Spelt
- Corn
- Oats
- Rye
- Buckwheat
- Rice
- Wild Rice
- Teff

Instead of wheat (whole or white) you can use spelt flour to make all your baked goods.

Modern wheat is the most difficult grain to digest and should be avoided by most people.

Wheat creates many blocks which increase inflammation throughout the body, especially in the digestive system. Dr. Pankaj Naram strongly recommends replacing wheat with any of the above-mentioned grains/flours. Due to its similarity in taste and texture to wheat, sorghum or spelt can be a good substitute for all forms of wheat. (*For people with gluten intolerance, spelt and rye should also be avoided in favor of other grains). Avoid whole wheat, white flour, all- purpose flour, cake flour, wheat crackers, store bought cookies, most breakfast cereals, thickeners, and many snack foods made from wheat.

Teff is Gluten-Free and Nutritious

The common English names for teff are teff, lovegrass, and annual bunch grass. Teff is an ancient grain, gluten free, the smallest grain in the world, and packed with nutrition. Because the grains of teff are so small, the bulk of the grain consists of the bran and germ. This makes teff nutrient dense as the bran and germ are the most nutritious parts of any grain. This grain has a remarkably high calcium content, and contains high levels of phosphorus, iron, copper, aluminum, barium, and thiamin.
It is considered to have an excellent amino acid composition, with lysine levels higher than wheat or barley. Teff is very high

in protein, carbohydrates, and fiber. The grain has been widely cultivated and used in the countries of Australia, Ethiopia, and India and its colonies. Teff is grown primarily as a cereal crop in Ethiopia where it is ground into flour and used for baking purposes. It is also eaten as porridge.

At this time, it is not widely known or used in the U.S., though it is cultivated in South Dakota, Idaho, Nevada, and California, and is available in many health-food stores. The color of the teff grains can be ivory, light tan to deep brown, dark reddish-brown, or purple, depending on the variety. Teff has a mild, nutty, and a slight molasses-like sweetness. The white teff has a chestnut-like flavor and the darker varieties are earthier and taste more like hazelnuts. Teff is a very versatile grain.

Teff flour can be used as a substitute for part of the flour in baked goods, or the grains may be added uncooked or substituted for part of the seeds, nuts, or other small grains. It is a good thickener for soups, stews, gravies, and puddings, and can also be used in stir-fry dishes, and casseroles.

Teff may be added to soups or stews in either of two ways:

1) Add them uncooked to the pot a half-hour before serving time.

2) Add them cooked to the pot 10 minutes before serving.

Cooked teff can be mixed with herbs, seeds, beans or tofu, garlic, and onions to make grain burgers. The seeds can also be sprouted, and the sprouts used in salads and on sandwiches.

To cook teff, place 2 cups purified water, 1/2 cup teff, and 1/4 tsp. sea salt (optional) in a saucepan. Bring to a boil, reduce heat and simmer, covered, for 15 to 20 minutes or until the water is absorbed. Remove from heat and let stand covered for 5 minutes.

Teff should be stored in a cool, dark, dry place in tightly covered containers such as glass jars.

About Nightshades

What? No white potatoes?
No tomatoes? No peppers?

According to Siddha-Veda, nightshades tend to irritate joints and the liver. Nightshades are difficult to digest because of their natural insect repellent, can disturb Doshas, and can overtax the digestive fire. Additionally, the toxicity increases with the addition of cheese.

Nightshades get their name because they grow at night, absorbing 'deadly night energies.' They are viewed as increasing mental stress and anxiety due to their stimulating nature.

List of Nightshades to Avoid:

- White potatoes
- Tomatoes
- Tomatillos
- Tamarios
- Pepinos
- Pimentos
- Eggplant
- Bell peppers

- Chili peppers
- Cayenne pepper
- Paprika
- Tabasco sauce and similar red pepper spicy or hot sauces
- Belladonna (highly poisonous, deadly nightshade)

About Oils

Organic coconut oil, organic avocado oil, organic canola oil, and especially Ghee are best for cooking. Olive oil is beneficial when used in the extra-virgin form and drizzled on top of cooked veggies, but some studies caution that it is not suitable for high heat cooking. Opinions change; do your own research on this one.

Peanut and mustard oils are Pitta aggravating and should be avoided for people with Pitta constitution or Pitta imbalance. Margarine, lard, Crisco®, cooking sprays, and all imitation oils should be completely avoided.

About Refined Sugar

Someone recently asked me
what is wrong with sugar if
you are thin and trying to gain
weight. Would not the higher
calories be beneficial in those
cases?

According to Siddha-Veda there are six tastes
(Rasas): sweet, sour, salty, bitter, pungent, and
astringent, with sweet being the most important
one. The sweet taste is best when it comes from
sweet fruits, rice, grains, legumes, nuts and seeds,
Ghee, and some vegetables (beets, cooked carrots,
yams, etc.).

Sweet taste balances Vata and Pitta but
aggravates Kapha. The primary elements in the
sweet taste include earth and water. The associated
qualities (Gunas) include heavy, cold, oily, soft,
relatively difficult to digest, grounding, building,
and nourishing. Positive emotions for sweet taste
include love, sharing, compassion, joy, happiness,
and bliss.

Of all sweeteners, less processed sugars like
jaggery, locally grown organic honey, and organic
pure maple syrup are considered to have a peaceful
effect on our minds. One source says, "White sugar
is sweet, heating, and has a stimulating effect on

the body, aggravating all the Doshas (Vata, Pitta, and Kapha), creating strong outward-seeking desire combined with dullness, depression, and ignorance in the mind."

Refined sugar comes from processed sugar cane, corn, or sugar beets; it is typically a combination of glucose and fructose. The body quickly breaks down refined sugar, causing a quick rise in insulin and blood sugar. Because fruit has fiber, it breaks down sugar more slowly and you get more of a sensation of being full, unlike refined sugar that leaves you craving increasingly more.

Honey should never be heated or baked, should not be mixed with Ghee, and should not be given to children under the age of two.

About Spices

Spices aid in the digestion and absorption of nutrients and improve the flavor of foods. Food should be spiced to have an overall warming effect but not a hot effect. It is the overall effect of the combination of spices that is most important.

Cumin, coriander, fennel, and saffron should be used liberally.

Also enjoy black pepper, fresh ginger root and ginger powder, turmeric, cinnamon, cardamom, cloves, mustard seeds, fenugreek, and nutmeg. Dill, anise, basil (Tulsi), oregano, poppy seeds, marjoram, sage, mineral salt (unrefined sea salt); thyme, bay leaf, and Asafoetida (hing) may also be used.

NOTE: Please avoid hot spices (red chilies and cayenne pepper), especially if you are Pitta Dosha.

See Reference Guide for Spices in Hindi (p. 175) and English to Hindi with Notes (p. 178)

Well-Equipped Kitchen

- Elio

For Safety: A fire extinguisher or at least an extinguisher spray to extinguish small kitchen fires.

For Measuring and Directions:

- Cutting board (bamboo is excellent)
- Cutlery set (knife set with sharpener)
- Measuring spoons and cups
- Vegetable peeler
- Metal spatula
- Tongs
- Colander (strainer)
- Cheese cloth (for making Ghee)
- Parchment paper
- Rolling pin (roller)

For Mixing:

- Hand-held blender/food chopper
- Set of stackable mixing bowls (lids are nice options to have)
- Whisk
- Large wooden spoons and spatula
- For Top-of-the-Range (Stove) or Oven Cooking

- Copper or stainless-steel pots and pans with lids
- 9"X9" and 9"X12" roasting pans for the oven
- Round cake pans (optional)
- Kettle for boiling water (electric kettle is also an option)
- Tea pot with a tea ball for loose tea
- Nice to Have and for Storage
- Glass bowls with lids (nesting bowls save space)
- Shredder, grater, potato masher, corer, dicer
- Make do – use what you have, can afford, and build on the basics.

Sample Shopping List

With this list, you can make soups, smoothies, electrolytes, an energy drink, chocolate brownies, crackers, healthy bread and more!

My Ancient Secrets
Grocery List (sample)

Basmati rice

Whole moong &/or split moong dal (yellow or green)

Oils: Ghee, coconut oil, or avocado oil (unsalted butter if making Ghee)

Fresh, organic vegetables

Sweet fruits & beetroot

Coconut water, organic tea, pomegranate juice

Cardamom pods, fresh ginger, cloves, garlic, fennel, cumin

Jaggery powder, agave & maple syrup

Black beans, dark cocoa powder, dark chocolate chips

Almonds, sesame seeds, sunflower seeds, sorghum flour

Eggs, baking soda, tahini

List of Organic Vegetable Options: zucchini, squashes, pumpkin, leafy greens, spinach, mangold (chard), onion, garlic, carrots, capsicum, fresh ginger, French beans, green peas, snow peas (mange tout), asparagus, fennel, rutabaga (swede), broccoli, beetroot, celery, chicory, leeks, bottle gourd.

Home Remedies – Ayushakti

Your Ayushakti Vaidya will advise you which home remedies you need to take. You can share these home remedies with your friends and family for the conditions we have mentioned.

Condition	Home Remedy
Acidity, burning	20 munakka (black raisins) soaked overnight in ½ a glass of water. Smash & filter it and add powders of 1 tsp. Jeera (cumin), ½ tsp. Variyali (fennel), ¼ tsp. Shunti (dry ginger), ½ tsp. Yashtimadhu (licorice root powder), 1 tsp. Amla (myrobalan fruit or Indian gooseberry, Mix all and take 3 times a day.
Agni, low	½ tsp. cumin powder ½ tsp. ginger powder 1 pinch Asafoetida
Arthritis, joint pain, back pain, neck pain, knee pain, morning stiffness, shoulder pain.	1. 1 tsp. of castor oil with warm water before going to bed. 2. 1 tsp. turmeric powder, ¼ tsp. gin-ger, ½ tsp. fenugreek, ¼ tsp. Ajwain, 1 tsp. coriander, ½ tsp. garlic paste. Mix all the ingredients in half a glass of warm water and drink twice daily.

Condition	Home Remedy
Autoimmune or Immune balancing	One glass of fresh juice made from carrot, pomegranate, and beetroot. Add ½ tsp. organic turmeric (curcumin) powder and drink. Drink this juice twice a day.
Calcium Supplement	Daily take any two of the below items and you will have enough calcium to support your bones: - 100 grams amaranth (rajgira) cooked - 100 grams Ragi (red millet/ nachni) - 1 cup cooked spinach, daily - 1 Tbsp. white sesame seeds, 2/day - 4 almonds, twice a day - 200 grams cooked broccoli daily
Cholesterol (to reduce)	2 Tbsp. psyllium husk, 1 tsp. Methi (fenugreek) powder with 1 glass of water, twice a day. 1 clove of garlic on empty stomach in the morning)
Cold / Cough / Allergy/ Congestion and Sinuses	10 Indian Basil (Tulsi) leaves (can be substituted with western basil) + 2.5 cm long piece of fresh ginger – crush both and get the juice from it (approx. 1 - 2 tsp.) + honey 1 tsp. + black pepper powder ¼ tsp., Garlic juice ½ tsp. Take this mixture 2-3 times a day.

Condition	Home Remedy
Constipation	One teaspoon Ayushakti's Amrutadi powder with half glass warm water daily at night.
Detox for Toxicity	1 tsp. cumin seeds powder, 1 tsp. coriander seeds powder, ½ tsp. ginger powder, 1 tsp. fennel seeds powder- boil all above in 1 liter of water for 5-10 minutes and then put it in a thermos (to keep warm). Drink this tea throughout the day. Stay on a Kitchari or moong and vegetable diet only.
Diabetes	½ tsp. Turmeric Powder ½ tsp. Methi (fenugreek) Powder 1 tsp. Amla Powder (Indian Gooseberry) 1 tsp. Jamun Beej Powder (blackberry) Mix them dry and swallow the powder with water; best time to take this is in the morning on an empty stomach.
Eye Problems (burning, short sight, long sight, strain)	Take 5 cardamon pods & remove seeds; take on empty stomach. Cotton pads dipped in cold milk placed on the closed eyes for 15 minutes reduces burning sensation.

Condition	Home Remedy
Gas, Indigestion	1 tsp. Jeera powder (cumin), ½ tsp. Shunthi (ginger), ¼ tsp. Ajwain (carom or bishop's weed), ½ tsp. black salt, 1 pinch of Hing. Mix all in half a glass of water and have two times a day after food. If you have a lot of gas, have it 4 times a day.
High Blood Pressure; Marmaa for BP	½ a glass of white pumpkin juice daily on an empty stomach. Apply Ghee on temples, press Marmaa point on temples 6 times, 6 x a day
Hormonal Imbalance	¼ tsp. Ajwain powder (carom or bishop's weed) 1 tsp. cumin powder, 1 tsp. fennel seeds powder. Mix the above in ½ cup water and take it twice a day.
Low Kidneys, Oedema	1 tsp. barley (Jav) seeds. Boil it with 2 cups of water and filter. Add 1 tsp. coriander powder, 1 tsp. cumin seed powder, ¼ tsp cardamom powder. Drink warm. Repeat this 3 times a day.

Condition	Home Remedy
Memory	1 tsp. Brahmi (Gotu kola) powder with ½ glass water daily. Or Ayushakti Sumedha 1 tablet, twice a day.
Metabolism, to Improve	1 tsp. dry ginger powder (Shunthi). Boil in 1 liter water for 5-10 minutes and then fill it in a thermos (to keep it warm). Drink little by little throughout the day to activate metabolism, burn fat and reduce congestion in the respiratory system.
Menstrual Bleeding, Excessive	1 tsp. cumin powder, 1 tsp. coriander powder, 4 pinches of alum powder, ½ tsp. raw sugar. Mix it in ½ a glass of water & drink mixture every hour.
Menstrual bleeding - scanty or no bleeding	1 tsp. cumin powder ½ tsp dill seeds powder ¼ tsp.. Ajwain powder (bishop's weed or carom) 1 tsp. jaggery Put in 1 cup (200 ml) of warm water and take it twice a day: after breakfast and after dinner.

Condition	Home Remedy
Mind, Peace of mind, recover from panic – Marmaa Points	1. Press center of both ear lobes 6 times. 2. Press the center of upper lip with index fingers 6 times. While doing this Marmaa, sit on a chair with your feet flat on the ground. 3. Head Marmaa: put ½ tsp. Ghee on the crown of your head and massage.
Neurological Tonic	White pumpkin juice - ½ glass daily
Polycystic Ovarian Disease (PCOD)	1 tsp. cumin ¼ tsp. Ajwain seed powder 1 pinch Asafoetida ¼ tsp. rock salt 1 tsp fennel ½ tsp. Saraca Indica (Asoka) Mix all well in half a glass of filtered water and drink 3 times a day. Take it for at least 6 months to 1 year.
Radiation Exposure	Triphala (three fruits powder), mint tea, turmeric. Diet of moong, healthy vegetables, and fresh, sweet fruits.
Sleep, Marmaa for sleep	Do cow's Ghee massage on both temples and both feet, 5–10 min before going to bed at night

Condition	Home Remedy
Sperm Count, Increase	1. 25 grams (¼ cup) cooked urad (black lentil) Dhal daily. 2. Juice from 2 fresh amla (myrobalan fruit, also called Indian Gooseberry fruit). 3. 2 deseeded dates filled with Ghee on an empty stomach in the morning. Good to take all three, if possible, at least for 6 months.
Stamina, energy, and increasing iron & calcium levels naturally	6 almonds + 2 dry figs + 2 dates + 2 cardamoms + 2 walnuts + 1 tsp. fennel seeds Soak all the above in a glass of water overnight. In the morning, deseed the dates, peel the almonds and cardamom. Crush all in a blender with water or almond milk and make a smoothie. Drink it first thing in the morning. Have breakfast only when you get hungry.

We hope these remedies are helpful. Keep in mind the wisdom of Master Jivaka: medicine for one person can be poison for another.

Everyone is unique and different. If you have questions on the remedies please consult an Ayushakti Vaidya or attend a Pulse Reading Clinic near you or book a video consultation with a trained Practitioner of the Ancient Secrets.

http://www.AncientSecretsFoundation.org/consultation

(When booking through this link, money is automatically donated for the orphan homes in Nepal).

Live Pulse Consultations (expressing interest is free, booking a consultation has a fee): To get on the waiting list for pulse clinics, and/or express interest in hosting a pulse, complete this form:

https://forms.gle/7AwjTJqK77wMkFzK6

Overview of Different Diets

Consult with your Vaidya, physician, or dietitian before starting major dietary changes, especially if you are taking prescription medication, are pregnant, or have chronic illness. No diet is right for everyone; consider your Dosha balance: Vata, Pitta, and Kapha.

Type of Diet	Directions
Diet for burning toxins, blockages and to reduce weight	**Step One:** 1-2 days ginger water diet. (2 tsp. of dry ginger powder added to 5 glasses of water. Bring it to a boil and drink warm throughout the day). **Step Two:** 3 days moong bean soup (soak one cup whole green gram (moong beans) overnight, pressure cook in the morning by adding 3 cups of water, garlic ginger paste, cumin powder, black pepper, salt, and garnish with coriander leaves. Make it in a soupy consistency and drink whenever you feel hungry throughout the day.

Type of Diet	Directions
	Step Three: 5 days moong soup and vegetables. (Pumpkin, zucchini, squashes, asparagus, carrots etc.) in the soaked moong, add enough water, spice it to your taste and cook well with a thick gravy consistency and drink throughout the day whenever you feel hungry for 5 days. **Step 4:** Then return to a normal diet but restrict your food proportion to 60% vegetables, 30% proteins and 10% carbohydrates. **List of Vegetables:** zucchini, squashes, pumpkin, leafy greens, spinach, mangold (chard), onion, garlic, carrots, capsicum, fresh ginger, French beans, green peas, snow peas (Mange- tout), asparagus, fennel, rutabaga (swede), broccoli, beetroot, celery, chicory and leeks, bottle gourd.

Type of Diet	Directions
Diet for hormonal imbalance	Have 60% vegetables, 30% protein, 10% carbohydrates. Avoid red meat, wheat, and sour, fried, or fermented food.
Detox diet	5-7 days of only moong and vegetables every month. You can eat items made from moong and vegetables whenever you are hungry for 3-5 times a day and eat nothing else. You can take coffee or tea, maximum 2 cups a day, preferably decaffeinated, without sugar or cream.
Tridosha Diet	• 1 Cabbage/Spinach • 2 Carrots • 1 Apple/Pomegranate. Make one glass of juice • Add half tsp. of organic turmeric powder Drink 3-6 glasses of juice every day.

Function of Key Herbs

Remember, everyone is different. Medicine for one person can be poison for another. Check with your Vaidya for additional information on how to use herbs for your specific Dosha and situation.

What	Herb & Description	Type	Additional Information
Brain	**Ashwagandha:** Improves brain function; helps with adrenal fatigue, healthy thyroid	Adaptogen	**Ashwagandha:** Balancing Vata and Kapha in excess, can imbalance Pitta & worsen Aam (toxic build up). Not for pregnant women. May interact with amitriptyline. Diuretic effect.
	Brahmi (water hyssop): Increases memory & focus, reduces anxiety and stress	Adaptogen; Antioxidant	
	Sage: Can improve brain function	Anti-microbial effect	

What	Herb & Description	Type	Additional Information
Heart	**Turmeric** Increases blood circulation; anti-inflammatory **Garlic:** Lowers bad cholesterol **Arjuna:** supports cardiovascular health **Green tea** (Camellia sinensis)	Diet and lifestyle as well as managing stress are vital to heart health	Turmeric (curcumin) may help with pain relief. It may thin your blood and make you bleed more easily. Avoid if taking warfarin (Coumadin).
Immunity	**Tulsi:** Helps fight infections and boosts immunity **Yarrow:** has astringent & anti-inflammatory properties; heals wounds	Holy Basil Achillea Millefolium Yarrow is good for skin wounds & bruises	Used in cough syrups & expectorants Yarrow has a mild sedative effect

What	Herb & Description	Type	Additional Information
Kidney	**Parsley:** Supports kidney functions **Marshmallow root:** acts as a diuretic	Serious kidney issues require help from a medical professio-nal or an Ayushakti physician	Avoid star fruit if uremic. The National Kidney Foundation lists these as not good for kidneys: alfalfa, aloe, bayberry, capsicum, cascara, ginger, ginseng, noni, senna, and more.

What	Herb & Description	Type	Additional Information
Liver	**Dandelion Root and Leaf:** (taraxacum officinale): Stimulates the flow of bile **Cardamom:** Detoxifies blood **Milk thistle (silymarin):** – may curb inflammation in the liver **Turmeric:** may be useful in treatment of hepatis B and C	Diet, weight and being free of alcohol are important to liver health	Look out for solvents and chemicals that can weaken the liver. Also be cautious of aloe vera, black cohosh, cascara, comfrey, green tea extract, ephedra, or kava. Some vitamins can also negatively affect the liver.

What	Herb & Description	Type	Additional Information
Lungs	**Peppermint** Acts as a decongestant; clears stag-nation. Soothes sore throat. Antispasmodic. **Cinnamon:** Gets rid of mucus		Aggravates vata Cinnamon also promotes healthy circulation & joints

What	Herb & Description	Type	Additional Information
Sto-mach	**Ginger:** Reduces gas & combats nausea; warming and calming **Peppermint:** (menthe piperita) – antispasmodic, for colic, spasms **Fennel:** Treats heartburn, gives energy, reduces sugar cravings **Cumin:** great for digestion, gas, constipation	Fennel is rich with anethole and fenchone, known to ease bloating and gas. Peppermint good for IBS	Ginger is also used for joint discomfort, motion sickness or air sickness. Ginger is contra-indicated for hyperacidity, during any form of hem-orrhage age, vertigo, and chronic skin disease.

Common Ingredients: Hindi to English

(including benefits of herbs)

Hindi Name	English Name	Notes
Ajwain	Celery (Thymol) Seeds	Carom Seeds
Adrak	Fresh Ginger	
Alsi	Flaxseed	
Amchoor	Mango Powder	
Anardana	Pomegranate Seeds	
Ata	Wheat Flour	
Badi Elaichi	Cardamom (Black)	
Besan	Gram Flour (chickpea flour)	Made from chana dal
Buna	Roasted Gram	
Channa	Chickpeas	Key ingredient in hum-mus & chana masala
Chana Dal	Bengal Gram Dal	
Dalchini	Cinnamon	
Dania	Coriander Seeds	
Elaichi	Cardamom (Green)	

Hindi Name	English Name	Notes
Haldi	Turmeric Powder	
Hing	Asafoetida	
Jaiphal	Nutmeg	
Jeera	Cumin Seeds	Seeragam (Tamil)
Kadi Patta	Curry Leaves	
Kali Mirch	Black Peppercorns	
Kasoori Methi	Dried Fenugreek Leaves	
Kesar	Saffron	Zaffran
Kuskus	Poppy Seeds	
Lahsun Powder	Garlic Powder	
Laung (Lavang)	Cloves	

Hindi Name	English Name	Notes
Maida	Flour	
Mehandi	Rosemary	
Methi Dana	Fenugreek Seeds	
Moong Dal	Green Gram	Also 'Mung'
Pippali	Long Pepper	
Poha	Rice Flakes	
Rava	Semolina	Cream of Wheat
Shunti	Dry Ginger	
Shotputpa	Fennel, Anisseed	Saunf
Subudana	Sago	
Sabut Moong	Whole Green Gram	
Sabza	Chia Seeds	
Tej Patta	Bay Leaf (dried)	
Thil	Sesame Seeds	
Til Oil	Gingelly oil/ sesame seed oil	
Tulsi	Holy Basil	
Tuvar Dal	Toor Dal/Yellow Lentil	
Urad Dal	Black Gram/ Black Lentil	
Zerra	Cumin	Jeera

Common Ingredients: English to Hindi

with Notes

English Name	Hindi Name	Notes
Asafoetida	Hing	May help lower blood pressure
Bay Leaf (dried)	Tej Patta	Protects against cancer, stress
Bengal Gram Dal	Chana Dal	Boosts energy, treats anemia
Black gram, black lentil	Urad Dal	Improved digestion, healthy heart, diabetes control, weight loss
Black Peppercorns	Kali Mirch	High in anti-oxidants, brain function
Cardamom (black)	Badi Elaichi	Heart health, skin & oral health
Cardamom (green)	Elaichi	Antioxidant & Diuretic
Celery (Thymol)	Ajwain	Carom Seeds: weight loss, heartburn, anti-inflammatory
Chia Seeds	Sabza	Antioxidants, fiber, protein

English Name	Hindi Name	Notes
Chickpeas	Channa	Key ingredient in hummus & chana masala
Cinnamon	Dalchini	Anti-viral, anti-bacterial, gut health
Cloves	Laung (Lavang)	Bone & Liver health, anti-oxidant, important nutrients
Coriander Seeds	Dania	Immune boosting anti-oxidants
Cumin	Zerra, Jerra	Antioxidants, anticancer, memory
Cumin Seeds	Jeera, Seeragam (Tamil)	Aids digestion, boosts immune system, expectorant
Curry Leaves	Kadi Patta	Improved digestion, weight loss
Dried Fenugreek Leaves	Kasoori Methi	Reduces risk of diabetes, reduces inflammation, pain relief
Dry Ginger	Shunti	Reduces obesity, digestion
Fennel, Anise Seed	Sanf, Saunf	Heart health, reduces Inflammation
Fenugreek	Methi	Anti-diabetic, pain relief

English Name	Hindi Name	Notes
Fenugreek Seeds	Methi Dana	Anticarcino-genic, hypo-glycemic effect on some people
Flaxseed	Alsi	Antidiabetic, Type II - may cause diarrhea, nausea, hormone issues
Flour	Maida	Naturally low in fat
Fresh Ginger	Adrak	Treats nausea, morning sickness
Garlic powder	Lahsun Powder Antica	Better blood pressure, lower bad cholesterol, for cold & flu
Gingelly oil (sesame seed oil)	Til Oil	Anti-inflamma-tory, treats arthritis; helps control blood sugar
Gram Flour (chickpea flour)	Besan, made from chana dal	Helps with acne, scars, and has zinc. Good for hair cleansing
Green Gram	Moong Dal, also mung	Heart health, antioxidant, reduces inflammation, treats diabetes
Holy Basil	Tulsi	Adaptogen, anti-inflammatory

English Name	Hindi Name	Notes
Long Pepper	Pippali	Caution for pregnancy & lactation
Mango Powder	Amchoor	Skin health, wellbeing, heart
Nutmeg	Jaiphal	Antioxidants, anti-inflammatory
Pomegranate Seeds	Anardana	Anti-inflammatory, anticarcino-genic, joint pain
Poppy Seeds	Kuskus	Thirst quenching minerals
Rice Flakes	Poha	Very nutritious, high-energy food
Roasted Gram	Buna	Anemia, anti-carcinogenic, digestion, feeling full
Rosemary	Mehandi	Antioxidant, anti-inflammatory, preventive for brain aging
Saffron	Kesar, Zaffran	Mood, PMS, digestion, may lower blood sugar
Sago	Subudana	May aid in weight gain, improves digestion

Conversion Table

MASS (Weight)	LENGTH
1 ounce (oz) = 28.0 grams (g)	¼ inch (in) = 0.6 centimeters (cm)
8 ounces = 227.0 grams	½ inch = 1.25 cm
1 pound (lb) or 16 ounces = 0.45 kg	1 inch = 2.5 cm
2.2 pounds = 1.0 kg	

LIQUID VOLUME	TEMPERATURE
1 teaspoon (tsp.) = 5.0 milliliters (ml)	212ºF = 100ºC
1 tablespoon (Tbsp.) = 15.0 ml	225ºF = 110ºC
1 fluid ounce (oz) = 30 ml	250ºF = 120ºC
1 pint (pt.) = 480 ml	275ºF = 135ºC
1 quart (qc.) = 0.95 liters (l)	300ºF = 150ºC
1 gallon (gal.) = 3.80 litres	325ºF = 160ºC
	350ºF = 180ºC
	400ºF = 200ºC
	420ºF = 220ºC
To convert temperature in Fahrenheit to Celsius, subtract 32 and multiply by .56	

PAN SIZES

8-inch cake pan = 20 x 4-cm cake pan
9-inch cake pan = 23 x 3.5-cm cake pan
11 x 7-inch baking pan = 28 x 18-cm baking pan
13 x 9-inch baking = 32.5x23-cm baking pan
9 x 5-inch loaf pan = 32.5 x 23-cm loaf pan
2-quart casserole = 2-liter casserole

Substitution Chart

Original	Healthy Version
All-Purpose Flour	Almond Flour, Sorghum, Millet, Chickpea
Bouillon Cubes	Vegetable stock, water
Breadcrumbs	Rolled Oats, Gluten-free Breadcrumbs
Butter	Solid Coconut Oil, Ghee
Caffeinated Tea	Herbal Teas
Cow's Milk	Almond, Oat, Coconut, or Rice Milk
Flour Tortillas	Corn Tortillas (gluten-free)
Pasta	Quinoa Pasta, Legume Pasta, Lentil Pasta, or Jerusalem Artichoke Pasta
Pizza Dough	Cauliflower Crust, Gluten-free Options
Salad Dressing	Extra Virgin Olive Oil & Wine Vinegar
Soda	Coconut Water
Table Salt	Sea Salt
Thickener / Starches	Arrowroot
White Potatoes	Sweet Potatoes
White Rice	Basmati Rice, Brown Rice
White Sugar	Palm Jaggery, Local Honey (don't heat), Maple Syrup, Date Sugar

Dosha Quiz - Ancient Secrets

In the book "Ancient Secrets of a Master Healer," legendary master healer, Dr. Naram, describes how all elements that exist in nature also exist in you (called 'Dosha' – "DOE-sha"). When they are balanced, you experience health. When they are imbalanced, you experience dis-ease.

By taking your pulse, practitioners of the ancient science can determine if you are predominantly one or the other or balanced: Tridosha. This helps the practitioner to understand what is happening in your body, mind, and emotions. It is used to determine what ailments you likely are suffering from or predict what you might be experiencing in the future.

It also helps them understand what food, herbs, home remedies, and lifestyle will be a kind of 'medicine' for you. Jivaka, physician for Buddha, said: "Everything can be a medicine or poison, depending on how you use it." (Ancient Secrets of a Master Healer, p. 55)

In the absence of having a consultation with a pulse healer/practitioner, you can get a general idea of what Dosha you might be most predominantly experiencing by answering the following simple questions...

How to Answer:

Answer each of the following three sections separately with numbers 1, 2, or 3. Put the number in the yellow column. Pick the number that best describes you in the past 90 days.

Everyone has some characteristics of all three Doshas; the balance or lack of balance gives us good information to help determine foods that work best with your constitution. You might find it interesting to have someone who knows you answer the questions for you and compare answers.

Sounds like me most of the time	3
Sometimes sounds like me	2
Seldom sounds like me	1
Total each column	
The column with highest number is your dominant dosha	

	Characteristic	Vata
Body Frame	Lean, delicate	
Skin	Dry, rough	
Appetite	Irregular appetite	
Weight	light	
Eyes	Small and active	
Hair	Brittle, dry, frizzy	
Joints	Thin, crackling, prominent	
Sleep	Light sleeper, awaken easily	
Body Temperature	Cold hands and feet	
Temperament	Lively, talkative, like change	
Stressed	Anxious, unfocused	
Focus	Likes to multitask	
Mood	Can change easily	
Instincts	Fight/Flight easily invoked	
	VATA TOTAL	

	Characteristics	Pitta
Body Frame	Medium build, muscular	
Skin	Prone to blemishes	
Appetite	Always hungry	
Weight	Moderate	
Eyes	Penetrating gaze	
Hair	Fine, thin, balding	
Joints	Loose & flexible	
Sleep	Moderately sound	
Body Temperature	Warm, like the cold	
Temperament	Purposeful, intense	
Stressed	Irritable & aggressive	
Focus	Goal oriented	
Mood	Strong emotions	
Instincts	Strong instincts and leadership	
	PITTA TOTAL	

	Characteristics	Kapha
Body Frame	Solid frame and thick bones	
Skin	Oily, smooth, few wrinkles	
Appetite	Can easily miss a meal	
Weight	Heavy, gains weight easily	
Eyes	Large, pleasant eyes	
Hair	Thick, luxurious, oily	
Joints	Large, padded, strong	
Sleep	Deep and long; awaken slowly	
Body Temperature	Moderate, don't like cold and wet	
Temperament	Easy going, accepting, supportive	
Stressed	Withdrawn, reclusive	
Focus	Slow to get started	
Mood	Calm and happy	
Instincts	Fight/Flight is not easily invoked	
	KAPHA TOTAL	

Eating for your Dosha Balance

Vata: Avoid dry snacks like crackers, popcorn, chips, cookies, or large amounts of raw foods. Enjoy a date shake, or guacamole with gluten-free bread, or an avocado.

Pitta: Long periods of fasting are not particularly beneficial for Pitta Dosha types. To decrease internal heat and fire, consider fresh sweet fruits, or small amounts of raw, organic vegetables like cucumber, zucchini, and carrot sticks. Also consider a handful of soaked and peeled almonds.

Kapha: Best to skip snacks altogether. Especially harmful to Kapha types are cold, wet foods, like ice cream, cold drinks, or oily.

Index

A

Aam, 24, **28**, 31, 56
About Beverages, 100
About Dairy and Eggs, 144
About Grains, 145
About Nightshades, 149
   - List of Nightshades to Avoid, 149
About Oils, 151
About Refined Sugar, 152
About Spices, 154
Acidity *(home remedy)*, 158
adaptogen, 169
ADD, 18
additives, 17
Aden, Ronney, 9, 65
ADHD, 18
Agni, **28**
   - low, 31
         (home remedy), 158
Allergy *(home remedy)*, 159
All Season Tea *(recipe)*, 104
almond milk, 37, 46, 102, 118, 164,
   183
Almond Milk: Homemade Raw *(recipe)*, 107
Amaranth, 145
amino acids, 56
Amodio, Katie, 6
Ancient Secrets Chocolate Frosting
   (recipe), 114
Ancient Secrets Community, vi
Ancient Secrets Foundation, x, 198
anise, 154
Anise Seed, 179
anti-cancer, 56
anti-inflammatory, 56
antimicrobial, 169
antioxidant, 169
antioxidants, 56
anxiety, 19, 77
Anxiety/Panic Marmaa, 163

Apple/Carrot/Beetroot Smoothie
   (recipe), 105
apples, 37, 43, 46
Apples, 50
arginine, 56
Arthritis *(home remedy)*, 158
Asafoetida, 154, 178
Ashtakarma/Panchakarma, 17
Ashwagandha, 169
Autoimmune (balancing) *(home remedy)*, 159
Ayurveda, 21
Ayushakti, xi, xiii, 1, 7, 72, 84, 86, 90,
   110, 136, 138, 158, 165, 171

B

Baked Pears with Goat's Cheese *(recipe)*, 121
Banana Coconut Oatmeal Cookies
   (recipe), 117
Basic Terms, **28**
   - Aam, 28
   - Agni, 28
   - Dhatus, 28
   - Doshas, 29
   - Gunas, 29
   - Ojas, 30
   - Srotas, 30
basil, 33, 65, 66, 93, 96, 154
Basil Herb Tea *(recipe)*, 103
bay leaf, 154
bay leaf (dried), 178
beetroot, 39, 80, 105, 136, 157
Beetroot-Finger Millet Pancakes
   (recipe), 39
Bengal Gram Dal, 178
Beverages
   - All Season Tea, 104
   - Almond Milk: Homemade Raw,
     107
   - Apple/Carrot/Beetroot Smoothie,
     105

Congratulations on choosing to love yourself through tasty, healthy food!

The recipes in this book are Ancient Secrets principles that can change your life forever.

To discover more about the Ancient Secrets, please visit:

www.MyAncientSecrets.com

For more recipes beyond this book and videos on how to make many of the recipes here, please visit our recipe sharing site: www.MyAncientSecrets.com/recipes

Proceeds from this book go to support orphans, homeless, and other humanitarian projects through Ancient Secrets Foundation. To find out more, you can visit: www.AncientSecretsFoundation.org

Book Cover Design – Courtesy of Heidi Aden, Lions Pen
LionsPenGraphics.com

Carol Ray and Dr. Clint Rogers, singing and playing with "Our Kids" in Nepal, 2023.

**Below "Our Kids" saying,
"I love you and I am with you!"**

Made in the USA
Las Vegas, NV
01 November 2024

10964974R00125